CANADIAN COOKING COMPANION

WILEY

JOHN WILEY & SONS CANADA, LTD

Toronto • New York • Chichester • Weinheim • Brisbane • Singapore

ISBN: 0-471-64380-7

Printed and Bound in Canada

10 9 8 7 6 5 4 3 2

Introduction

The Canadian Cooking Companion was created to provide student chefs with the information they need regarding the grading and inspection of food in Canada. It wil also help them respond to the increased interest in healthy eating by introducing them to the basics of nutrition and vegetarian cuisine and fish and seafood products available in Canada.

The Companion is divided into five modules, each featuring an introductory 'Learning Guide' and concluding summary and review material. Each module was written by a Canadian chef-educator and explains the topic covered in a manner that will be accessible to beginning students.

The modules are as follows:

1. Nutrition in Canada
2. Meat Inspection and Grading In Canada
3. Poultry and Egg Inspection and Grading in Canada
4. Canadian Fish and Seafood
5. Culinary Arts and Vegetarianism

Contents

1

Nutrition

by Albert Cipryk

What's in it for us

• Do you want to have a better understanding of the concepts of nutrition?

• Do you want to explore the topics that will make you aware of the route to healthier eating?

• Do you want to learn some guidelines in running a more nutrition friendly kitchen?

This module will provide you with a basic introduction to nutrition. Note that the information presented is not in-depth and discusses just briefly, the major factors of nutrition. This module lists some examples of nutrition media, preparation techniques related to healthier cooking and tips toward a more nutrition friendly menu.

Learning Guide

Goal: The purpose of this module is to provide an overview of the basic principles of nutrition.

Learning Outcome: After completing this module, you will be able to identify some of the factors and concerns pertaining to healthy nutrition.

Learning Objectives: As you work through this module you will learn to:

1. Understand the language of nutrition such as the definition of calorie, carbohydrate, fat, protein, vitamins, minerals and trace elements.
2. Understand the desired balance of energy in and energy out.
3. Understand the Canada Food Guide approach to healthy eating and examine the Mediterranean Pyramid diet.

Introduction

"You are what you eat." This was a phrase coined by people who realized that nutrition was the lifeline to healthy living.

We are an assembly of molecules. From conception, this collection of molecules increases at a staggering rate to form an incredible machine, the human body. Able to think and reason, able to walk, speak and perform a myriad of tasks, the human body strives for maturity, linked to one undeniable input, nutrition.

Our approach to nutrition is to study how humans, through food, ingest, digest, metabolize, assimilate, transport and store the nutrients necessary to enable our bodies to grow and maintain healthy structures.

Our knowledge of nutrition has increased tremendously in the last few years. In developing nations, nutrition has been and remains a life and death situation. For all our knowledge, much of the planet endures a subsistence living; underfed and undernourished. In North America we see, perhaps, a stranger anomaly; that of many thousands of people who are overfed and undernourished.

Through high calorie snacks and between meal treats, we have no problem in loading up on calories. The problem, of course, is that they are "empty" calories, bereft of all but minimal nutrient value. The lesson of sound nutritional habits seems to be a difficult one to learn.

The purpose of this chapter is not to make nutritionists of you. It is hoped, that you will become aware of the importance and the need of understanding the principles of good nutrition; what is required to ensure that your daily dietary intake will be ample and sufficiently varied to maintain a healthy lifestyle.

A chef with this information is more likely to create menus and recipes that provide healthier choices.

For too long, the food service industry was thought to be doing less than its fair share of educating the public about healthy eating habits.

It appears, however, that there is a pinpoint of light at the end of the tunnel. Increasingly, the call to chefs today is to provide a selection of carefully planned menu items whose nutritional content is lower than normal in saturated fats, cholesterol and sodium. A healthier menu.

Armed with the correct nutritional information, today's chefs in training will more easily heed the call.

The Science of Nutrition

Science dictionaries define nutrition as: The science of food, the nutrients, and other substances therein, their action, interaction, and balance in relation to health and disease, and the processes by which the organism ingests, digests, absorbs, transports, utilizes and excretes food substances.

That is fine as far as it appears, but just what does it really mean. Let's break the definition down piece by piece. Nutrition examines food and the other substances within it.

Nutrients are the constituent parts of the food necessary to supply energy and maintain a healthy body. Therefore, they are essential to life.

Nutrients can be categorized as macronutrients which include those of carbohydrate, fat, protein and water. Micronutrients are the vitamins, minerals and trace elements.

Additional non-nutritional substances in foods may be preservatives, additives, naturally occurring toxins and environmental contaminants.

Looking around a summer market or supermarket leaves one wondering how it is possible in our society to have a nutrient deficiency. However, what we see and what may be the truth about our nutritional habits can be vastly different.

It is sobering to think that according to research, up to 25 percent of our daily calories can come from sugar, a main ingredient in many modern packaged foods. Sugar contains nothing besides calories. From this, we can see that immediately, one quarter of our diet is lost as a potential source of vitamins and minerals.

A typical modern diet may contain calories from processed fats—margarine, cooking oils, salad dressings, baking shortenings; all high in calories and minimal in nutrients, perhaps from 15 to 30 percent of daily calories.

Alcohol will add calories but at best has just traces of vitamins and minerals.

Here we sit with the technology that on one hand enables us to dine like royalty and on the other makes it possible to waste a substantial amount of our diet on food that would not nourish a lab rat.

The Language of Nutrition

CALORIE OR KCALORIE

A calorie is a unit by which energy is measured. Technically, a calorie is the amount of heat necessary to raise the temperature of one gram of water one degree centigrade. Food energy is measured in kilocalories (thousands of calories), abbreviated kcalories or kcal. A capitalized version is sometimes used: Calories. Most people, even nutritionists, speak of these units simply as calories, but on paper they are prefaced by a k.

Reference to calories or kcalories is not a reference to the make up of the food, but to the potential energy of that food.

Carbohydrates, fats and proteins can all be measured in kcalories when completely broken down. Carbohydrates will provide four kcalories per gram, as will a

gram of protein. However, one gram of fat is worth nine kcalories. The potential energy content of a specific food is dependent entirely upon the amount of carbohydrate, protein and fat it contains.

A principle consideration is what happens when your body does not use all of these nutrients to fuel the processes of metabolism and daily physical activity. The body will convert them and the energy they contain into a type of storage facility most commonly seen as body fat, to be used between meals and overnight.

Ideally we should spend as many calories through metabolism and exercise as we ingest. When there is an excess of calories taken in, regardless of whether they come from carbohydrate, fat or protein, they will end up stored as body fat, a weight gain. Too many protein rich steaks will end up in a calorie surplus as will too many carbohydrate rich potatoes.

Macronutrients

Macronutrients are those nutrients which supply the calories for energy. Of the big three, fats supply nine kcalories per gram and carbohydrate and protein four each.

CARBOHYDRATES

Carbohydrates have been unjustly maligned as the food that contributes most to weight gain. This is not true, of course, since excess amounts of any calorie bearing food will contribute to weight gain. Ask people what food they shy away from when dieting and too often the answer is potatoes and bread.

A chart of calorie counts of common foods shows that a medium size apple and potato have roughly the same number of calories, about 85-100. Why the misconception? It's easy, people do not usually put butter, sour cream and bacon bits on their apple. At the same time, they consider the fat laden garnish as part of the potato.

Carbohydrates supply us with that indispensable item of life, energy. Without sufficient carbohydrates in our diet, ideally about 60 percent of our calorie intake, our bodies would be converting protein to energy rather than using it for functions for which it is uniquely suited.

Carbohydrates are starches and sugars. They are found in such foods as bread, cereals, potatoes, pastas, rice, fruits, vegetables, milk, ice cream and yogurt. Carbohydrate is found predominately in plant foods. The only common animal source food containing significant amounts of carbohydrate is milk.

All carbohydrates are composed of simple sugars. The chemist's term for the three sugars are monosaccharides, disaccharides and polysaccharides. The first two are simple carbohydrates and the third is a complex carbohydrate. The body invariably converts carbohydrates, regardless of what form they come in (except fibres) into a form it can best use, blood sugar, properly termed glucose.

It is important to understand that excess intakes of refined sugars, such as those in packaged foods, supply a form of sugar but not additional healthful nutrients. Although this sugar is carbohydrate, it is made up of empty calories.

Quality carbohydrate is our fastest source of food energy. When we eat a meal the last thing to be digested are fats, the second last are proteins and the first are carbohydrates.

Carbohydrates are easily broken down into simple sugars that are turned into the blood sugar, glucose. Remember back to a time when you had a really large meal, such as Christmas dinner, comprised of turkey with glistening high fat skin, gravy with fat in its makeup, mashed potatoes with butter, buttered vegetables and high fat dessert. That full feeling which went on forever is due, largely to the high fat content of the meal. Carbohydrate converts into useable energy in a fraction of the time it takes to digest the other nutrients.

FIBRES

Fibre is another reason we need sufficient carbohydrate foods in our diet, particularly less refined carbohydrate. Fibre is to plants what bones are to animals. They help provide the structure to a plant's stems, leaves and fruits. Fibre is made up of cellulose and other complex carbohydrates that are not broken down by our digestive systems. This bulky material assists in moving digested material and water along our intestinal tracts clearing the body of the bulk of the material and especially of cancer causing toxic wastes produced through the process of digestion.

Based on the observations of physicians in Africa, the "fibre hypothesis" suggests that the consumption of unrefined, high-fibre, carbohydrate foods protects against many Western diseases, such as colon cancer and cardiovascular disease. Rural Africans naturally consume a diet very high in fibre and show a low incidence of many chronic conditions.

High fibre foods may also play a role in weight control. According to the fibre hypothesis, obesity is not seen in those parts of the world where people eat large amounts of fibre-rich foods. Foods high in fibre tend to be low in fat and simple sugars.

FATS

People tend to think that the less fat you have on your body and the less fat you have in your diet, the better off you are. This is not true. Everybody needs some fat. In fact, about 30 percent of our daily calories should come from fat. The body requires this supply for its constant manufacture of living cells; it needs fats combined with proteins to line the intestines, to sheath nerve cells, even to make brain tissue. Like all nutrients, fat is beneficial in appropriate quantities—and it is harmful to ingest either too much or too little of it. It is true, though, that in our society of abundance, people are more likely to encounter too much fat than too little.

Not only is fat important in the body, it is important in foods as well. Many of the compounds that give foods their flavour, aroma, and tenderness are found in fats and oils; they are fat soluble. When the fat is removed from a food, many of the fat soluble compounds are also removed. Significant among these are flavours and vitamins.

By carrying both flavour and aroma, fat lends palatability to foods. It is the fat that makes the delicious aromas associated with bacon, ham, hamburger and other meats, as well as onions being fried, French fries, and stir-fried vegetables. The attractiveness of fat is responsible for the popularity of fast foods, which, critics say, are too palatable for our own good. Fat also adds to that fullness feeling we get from foods, another reason fast foods are so popular.

Our most recent generation has leaned more on the information that excess fats in our diet, particularly saturated animal fats, tend to encourage cardiac disease. Today's dietary buzzwords always include cholesterol, monounsaturates, polyunsaturates and saturates. Of these, cholesterol seems to get the most publicity.

Simply put, cholesterol floats in our blood stream. It is a fat manufactured by our bodies and ingested in animal foods. When an excess amount is present either from our own bodies or from high amounts ingested through high cholesterol foods, the body cannot excrete the excess fully and it tends to accumulate on the arterial walls leading to the heart. Dense and deep accumulation of this arterial plaque re-

stricts blood flow to the heart which can lead to cardiac disease.

It is interesting to note that there is no cholesterol in any plant foods. As a general rule, anyone wishing to reduce both saturated fat and cholesterol intake could accomplish these objectives by selecting fish, poultry without skin, lean meats, and nonfat milk products; choosing vegetables, fruits, cereals, and legumes; and limiting oils, fats, egg yolks, and fried foods.

PROTEIN

Protein is probably the most commonly known of the nutrients. Everybody knows we have to have protein. Magazine ads tout protein supplements showing photographs of incredibly sculpted muscle builders whose destiny resides in the package of protein in their hand.

The image of protein is muscle building. Protein suggests power and strength. Protein is big steaks and red meat. Right? Well, not necessarily so. Protein is available in a variety of foods most commonly available.

We all need protein. Protein is necessary for the constant building and rebuilding of every cell in our bodies. It and other nutrients are used in the performance of the various functions of the body. However, protein as a nutrient and meat as a source have been frequently overvalued so that people eat much more than they normally need.

Of all the calories you need in a day, only 10 percent need be from protein. An understanding of the quantity and quality of protein one needs is important in achieving the correct proportions of nutrients in a balanced diet.

Protein is a chemical compound that contains the same atoms as carbohydrate and fats; carbon, hydrogen, and oxygen, but protein is different in that it also contains nitrogen atoms. It is this added nitrogen atom which enables the protein to be arranged in to amino acids, the building blocks of protein.

There are twenty amino acids important to human nutrition. Of these, nine cannot be manufactured by the body, and therefore, they must be provided by the diet.

For this reason, it is essential that a balanced diet be achieved for proper health. Not all protein based foods contain "complete" protein. That is, not all contain the twenty amino acids important to human nutrition. Meats are an excellent source of complete protein.

For vegetarians who derive their dietary protein from nuts, legumes, vegetables and other non-animal foods, special care must be taken since many of these foods are incomplete proteins; that is, they do not contain the complete requirement of amino acids. In this case, complete protein can be achieved by eating more than one protein source which in combination will provide the nutrients necessary to form complete proteins.

There are many examples of high and low quality protein, the terms used to refer to those proteins which are complete or incomplete. Animal based proteins (meat, fish, poultry, eggs and milk) tend to be uniformly complete. Some plant foods are notoriously incomplete, for example, corn protein. Some, however, are complete, such as the protein of rice and potatoes.

We can get high nutritional value proteins by combining foods. For example, the cereal proteins in bread, buns, pastas and breakfast cereals are of low quality, mainly because they contain very little of the essential amino acid lysine. Lysine is in plentiful quantity in legume proteins, as in beans, peanuts and soybeans. So, if we combine a cereal-protein food like bread with a legume-protein food like peanut butter we produce a food of high nutritional quality: the peanut butter sandwich.

Completeness of protein is not the only issue of concern with respect to protein quality. For the highest quality, proteins must be not only complete but also digestible, so that sufficient numbers of their amino acids reach the body's cells to permit them to make the proteins they need.

WATER

Of all the nutrients required by the human body, none will cause the whole system to shut down as quickly as the lack of water. It is also the most plentiful of the nutrients. Even when drinking milk or juice, we are drinking mainly water. Milk is 88 percent water and so is orange juice. We ingest water through solid foods such as hard cheese. Cucumbers and watermelon are about 95 percent water.

The body fluids provide the medium in which all of the cells' chemical reactions take place. The water based fluids participate in many of these reactions and supply the means for transporting vital materials to cells and carrying waste products away from them. Sufficient water is necessary to ensure that our digestive system operates properly from the assimilation of nutrients to the elimination of waste. Insufficient water can easily halt the smooth elimination of digestive waste and cause great discomfort and constipation.

Water is the main component of the body and accounts for up to two-thirds of its weight. Fortunately for us, our bodies are equipped with a thirst regulating mechanism in the brain that tells us when our bodies need water. We automatically feel thirsty and drink. We constantly need to replenish our water supply since through urinating, perspiring, breathing and regular body metabolism, the supply is constantly being depleted.

Water based body fluids:
• carry nutrients and waste products

throughout the body fill the cells and the spaces between them
- help to form the structure of macromolecules
- participate in chemical reactions
- serve as solvents for minerals and vitamins
- act as lubricants around joints
- serve as shock absorbers inside the eyes, spinal cord and protect the baby during pregnancy
- aid in the body's temperature regulation

There are times when the greatest favour you can do for your body is to turn on the tap and have a long, cold drink.

Micronutrients

Micronutrients are those essential nutrients which cannot be manufactured by the body and are ingested into the body in small quantity. Micronutrients include vitamins, minerals and trace elements. Micronutrients contain no calories.

VITAMINS

Vitamins differ from carbohydrates, fats and proteins in that they do not yield energy when broken down but assist enzymes with energy production and help cells multiply for growth and healing.

Vitamins are organic in makeup and as such are destructible. Care must be taken in their cooking to maintain as much nutrient value as possible in the finished product.

Each vitamin plays a variety of roles in the bodily function.

VITAMIN A

The most important function of vitamin A in the body is in forming and keeping healthy the epithelial tissue, which is the shield the body forms to protect it from infections and other external hazards. Skin is epithelial tissue as are mucous linings of the mouth and intestines. Vitamin A is also essential to maintaining good night vision.

The major source of vitamin A in our diets is yellow and green vegetables as well as liver, kidney, eggs and whole milk.

VITAMIN B

Vitamin B1 (thiamin) is needed for the metabolism of carbohydrates, and the more carbohydrates we eat, the more thiamin we need. Thiamin is found in pork cuts, beef cuts, liver and in whole grain or enriched bread or cereal. Thiamin deficiency may result in damage to the nervous and cardio-vascular system and muscle wastage.

Vitamin B2 (riboflavin) helps enzymes to facilitate the release of energy from nutrients needed in every cell of the body. No specific disease is associated with riboflavin deficiency. Lack of the vitamin affects the facial skin with cracks and redness forming near the corners of the eyes and lips as well as other symptoms.

Most common foods supplying riboflavin are meats, fish and poultry, vegetables and milk products.

The B Vitamin niacin is involved in the release of energy from carbohydrates, fats, or proteins. It acts in close association with thiamin and riboflavin. The higher the caloric intake, the greater the need for niacin. The main dietary sources of niacin are meats, poultry and seafoods, fruit and vegetables.

Niacin deficiency is associated with the disease, pellagra, which symptoms include dermatitis, diarrhea and dementia. Pellagra was rampant in the U. S. south during the 1800s and early 1900s because of a low protein diet whose staple grain was corn. This diet was unusual in that it supplied neither enough niacin nor enough of its appropriate amino acid to make up the deficiency.

Vitamin B6, pyridoxine is required for the metabolism of proteins including absorption of amino acids in the intestines and their transport from tissue to tissue in the body. Our body's need for pyridoxine depends on the amount of protein we eat. The more protein we consume; the more pyridoxine we need.

Good sources of pyridoxine are legumes, whole grain cereals and bread, various fruits and various cuts of meat. Other B vitamins required in our regular diets are Biotin, Folacin, Pantothenic acid and cobolamin. These are available through a healthy diet of various fruits, vegetables and meats.

VITAMIN C

Vitamin C figures popularly in the stories of the 1700s sailors falling ill with scurvy and the resulting discovery that limes or other citrus fruits (those high in vitamin C) could cure the condition. To this day, British sailors who were first given "the cure" are known as "limeys".

Vitamin C is needed for the metabolism of proteins and many amino acids. It is also important to the absorption of iron from the intestine and to the storage of iron in the liver.

Vitamin C deficiency results in many signs of tissue damage, particularly the connective tissue that holds skin, muscles, tendons and bones together. This shows up in the form of bleeding gums, delayed healing of burns and wounds, and hemorrhaging of small blood vessels causing red spots under the skin.

Research has shown that recovery from the common cold seems easier with sufficient amounts of Vitamin C and has been established that smoking causes depletion of Vitamin C in the body.

At one time megadoses of Vitamin C were popularized as a cure for many common ills. There does not seem to be any scientific basis for this position. It has been shown, however, that megadoses of Vitamin C have caused nausea, abdominal cramps and diarrhea. Extreme doses of

Vitamin C excreted in the urine have also been known to obscure the results of tests used to detect diabetes.

A very wide variety of fruits and vegetables provide sufficient amounts of Vitamin C in our diets.

VITAMIN D

Vitamin D is essential for forming bone and keeping it strong. Bone is made from calcium and phosphorus. Vitamin D helps the absorption and utilization of calcium and phosphorus.

Except for the Vitamin D added to milk, food contains very little Vitamin D. We take in Vitamin D from sunshine and through enriched milk which has the addition of Vitamin D in North America and many European countries. Years ago the common Vitamin D supplement taken in winter was cod liver oil. Although this is still available, its appearance in processed milk has all but replaced the liver oil product.

VITAMIN E

Vitamin E is one of the most talked about vitamins. To some people Vitamin E is a miracle drug curing arthritis, ulcers, acne, heart disease and infertility. To scientists Vitamin E seems to be a first line of defense in protecting vulnerable components of cells from oxidation which would interfere with its ability to perform its particular function.

High doses of Vitamin E have been known to interfere with the effectiveness of certain prescription drugs.

Food sources of Vitamin E are quite common. These include salad oils, shortenings and spreads as the main sources with fruits, vegetables and grains supplying smaller amounts.

VITAMIN K

Vitamin K seems to have one chief function and that is to make blood clot. Obviously its presence can mean the difference between life and death. At least 13 different proteins and the mineral calcium are involved in making a blood clot. Vitamin K is essential for the synthesis of at least four of these proteins.

Food sources rich in Vitamin K are all green leafy vegetables, eggs, soybean oil and liver.

MINERALS

For all the good the vitamins we have examined above do for us, none of them are of any benefit without the accompaniment of minerals. The balance of minerals in the body is so critical that the imbalance can cause the body to shut down, resulting, in some cases, coma and even death. At best, only a partial list of the function of each of the minerals can be given.

PHOSPHORUS

Most of the phosphorus our bodies require goes to form bones and teeth. The balance (about 15-20 percent) is used in soft tissues. Phosphorus aids in protein formation, in transferring hereditary characteristics from one generation of cells to another and to metabolize carbohydrates.

There is very little problem getting enough phosphorus in our diets. Foods rich in phosphorus include whole-grain cereal and bread, legumes, nuts, dairy products, meat, fish and poultry.

CALCIUM

Ninety-nine per cent of the calcium in the body is in the bones. The other one per cent labours away in the blood and other fluids and in soft tissue. Calcium works with vitamin K to help blood clotting when necessary and also helps with muscle tone and nerve function.

Foods rich in calcium are hard cheeses, dark green leafy vegetables, fish with soft bones such as tinned salmon and sardines, legumes, nuts and eggs.

IRON

Iron is an essential component in the process by which cells produce energy. Every human cell contains iron. Iron is also found in many enzymes that oxidize compounds, and is required for the making of new cells, of amino acids and hormones. Because so much of the body's iron is in the blood, iron losses are greatest whenever blood is lost. Women's menstrual losses make a woman's iron needs twice as great as a man's, but anyone who loses blood, even through a blood donation, loses iron. Women are more prone to iron deficiency since they are generally smaller and take in less food.

Foods rich in iron include meat (particularly liver), shellfish, spinach, legumes, eggs, whole-grain breads and cereals.

SODIUM AND POTASSIUM

Sodium and potassium belong together. They act in balance to maintain a normal flow of nerve signals and muscle contractions. Sodium and potassium also play a role in maintaining a balance between the acids and bases in our body fluids. Sodium is further needed for the absorption of various nutrients, while potassium is needed for energy release from carbohydrates, fats and proteins. Both tend to act to regulate blood pressure.

Both sodium and potassium are plentiful in our food supply. Sodium is found in table salt which we add to foods. It is also present in fruits, vegetables and milk. Potassium-rich foods are bananas, oranges, tomatoes, potatoes plus other fruits and vegetables.

MAGNESIUM

Half the magnesium in our bodies is in the bones and teeth. The other half is in soft tissues, helping the release of energy from glycogen, the making of proteins, the regulating of body temperature and the orderly contraction of nerves and muscles. Magnesium is found in whole-grain bread and cereals, nuts, beans and green leafy vegetables.

ZINC

Zinc is used by the body in the formation of many hormones, including insulin, which regulates carbohydrate metabolism, and many enzymes, including those controlling the transport of carbon dioxide in the blood.

Good sources of zinc are animal foods such as meat, liver, eggs and shellfish, particularly oysters.

IODINE

Our bodies have what is known as a basal metabolic rate, a minimum level of life processes. Iodine is a key factor in regulating basal metabolic rate as well as other body functions.

Adequate supplies of iodine are not a problem since table salt is iodized. Additional iodine appears in seafood and in fruits and vegetables grown near the seashore where salt is more prevalent because of the influence of sea water.

FLUORIDE

The most common association with fluoride is that of dental health and maintenance. However, the value of fluoride extends beyond the prevention of dental caries. Not only is fluoride deposited in the enamel of the teeth to strengthen it against decay, but it is also deposited in the crystals of the bones, extending their healthy life and possibly warding off the onset of osteoporosis, a degenerative bone disease.

Fluoride is most effective when ingested rather than applied topically as with fluoride toothpaste. Very small quantities of fluoride are present in our most common foods and the best access to it is through municipal fluoridated water supplies.

TRACE ELEMENTS

Of the fifty or so essential nutrients and chemicals required by the body to work in perfect harmony, some are required in such minute quantities that we see their amounts as just a trace in the overall picture. It is almost easier to see what happens in the absence of one of these elements rather than what function it actually performs.

Barely measurable amounts of copper, cobalt, molybdenum, selenium, vanadium and others all work to keep us healthy and functioning happily.

These trace elements or trace minerals are all available in regular diets.

Energy In, Energy Out

By careful calculation we can account for all the food we take in during a day and convert it into potential energy with a calorie count. We know that fats have ninekcalories per gram and protein and carbohydrates have four each. But to maintain the fine balance of energy in and energy out, you also need to know your expenditure. The easiest way to determine how much energy you are "burning" is to use established charts for the "typical" Canadian citizen.

The Canadian ministry of health, Health Canada, has published recommended energy intakes for various age-sex groups as well as charts estimating energy spent on various activities.

ENERGY IN

A typical 20 year old woman, for example, 165 cm tall and weighing 58 kilograms needs about 2200 kcalories a day to maintain her weight. The healthy 20 year old man used as a reference figure stands 178 cm tall and weighs 73 kg. His recommended caloric intake is about 2900 kcalories. The assessment is done assuming normal daily activity. Increased activity would naturally call for a higher daily intake of calories. A span of 500-800 calories should accommodate any fluctuation of daily energy needs.

ENERGY OUT

The following chart is an example of the rate at which average young adults burn calories during various activities.

Activity	Kcalories per hour
Brisk walking	300 kcalories per hour
Jogging	600 kcalories per hour
Swimming	500 kcalories per hour
Cross country skiing (uphill)	1150 kcalories per hour
Sitting (loafing)	100 kcalories per hour

MAINTAINING THE BALANCE

In order to maintain a constant body weight, balance must be maintained between the number of kcalories you take in and the number of kcalories you expend.

SHIFTING THE BALANCE

A pound (450 g) of body fat stores about 3,500 kcalories. To lose it, you must take in 3,500 kcalories less than you expend; to gain it, you must take in 3,500 kcalories more than you use. On the average, a deficit or excess of 500 kcalories a day brings about a weight loss or gain, respectively, at the rate of one pound (450 g) a week; a deficit or excess of 1,000 kcalories a day, two pounds (900 g) per week. Losing one pound (450 g) in one week can be achieved by expending 500 kcalories per day in excess of your daily intake for seven

days; (7 x 500 = 3,500 kcalories).

How you choose to make up the daily 500 kcalories is up to you. The straightforward method would be to either eat less or do more. Another way would be to pass up a 200 kcalorie dessert and take a brisk, one hour, 300 kcalorie walk. The combinations are endless and could end up being very interesting.

How do you know that you are getting the proper nourishment with the proper variety of foods in the proper amounts?

Health Canada's "Food guide to healthy eating" is a simple and direct way to access the information needed to ensure that you are eating a healthy, balanced diet.

Canada's Guidelines For Healthy Eating

1. Enjoy a ***variety*** of foods.
2. Emphasize cereals, breads, other grain products, vegetables and fruits.
3. Choose lower-fat dairy products, leaner meats and foods prepared with little or no fat.
4. Achieve and maintain a healthy body weight by enjoying regular physical activity and healthy eating.
5. Limit salt, alcohol and caffeine.

You don't have to give up foods you love for the sake of your health. But you do need to aim for variety and moderation. Let Canada's Food Guide to Healthy Eating help you make your choices.

Health Canada   Santé Canada

CANADA'S
Food Guide

TO HEALTHY EATING
FOR PEOPLE FOUR YEARS
AND OVER

Enjoy a variety
of foods from each
group every day.

Choose lower-
fat foods
more often.

Grain Products
Choose whole grain
and enriched prod-
ucts more often.

Vegetables and Fruit
Choose dark green and
orange vegetables and
orange fruit more often.

Milk Products
Choose lower-fat milk
products more often.

Meat and Alternatives
Choose leaner meats,
poultry and fish, as well
as dried peas, beans
and lentils more often.

Canada

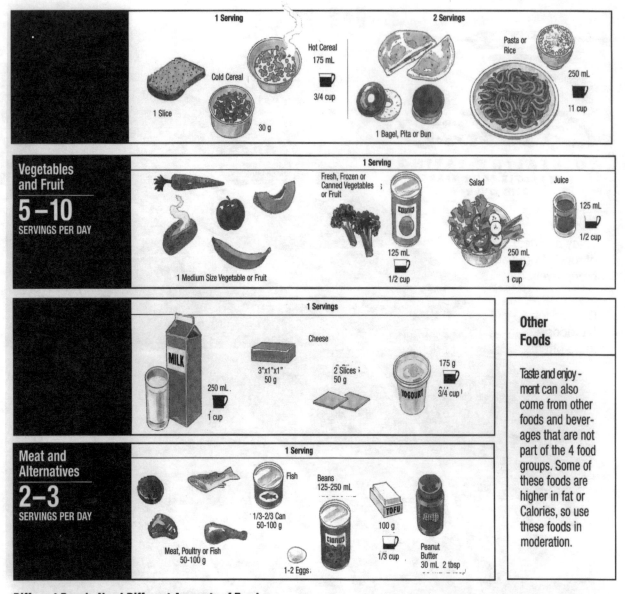

1 Serving

Cold Cereal

Hot Cereal
175 mL
3/4 cup

1 Slice

30 g

2 Servings

Pasta or
Rice

250 mL
11 cup

1 Bagel, Pita or Bun

Vegetables and Fruit

5 – 10
SERVINGS PER DAY

1 Serving

Fresh, Frozen or
Canned Vegetables
or Fruit

Salad

Juice

125 mL
1/2 cup

1 Medium Size Vegetable or Fruit

125 mL
1/2 cup

250 mL
1 cup

125 mL
1/2 cup

1 Servings

MILK

250 mL
1 cup

Cheese

3"x1"x1"
50 g

2 Slices
50 g

YOGOURT

175 g
3/4 cup

Other Foods

Taste and enjoy-
ment can also
come from other
foods and bever-
ages that are not
part of the 4 food
groups. Some of
these foods are
higher in fat or
Calories, so use
these foods in
moderation.

Meat and Alternatives

2 – 3
SERVINGS PER DAY

1 Serving

Fish

1/3-2/3 Can
50-100 g

Beans
125-250 mL

Meat, Poultry or Fish
50-100 g

1-2 Eggs

TOFU

100 g

1/3 cup

Peanut
Butter
30 mL 2 tbsp

Different People Need Different Amounts of Food

The amount of food you need every day from the 4 food groups and other foods depends on your age, body size, activity level, whether you are male or female and if you are pregnant or breast-feeding. That's why the Food Guide gives a lower and higher number of servings for each food group. For example, young children can choose the lower number of servings, while male teenagers can go to the higher number. Most other people can choose servings somewhere in between.

Enjoy eating well, being active and feeling good about yourself. That's

Mediterranean Food Pyramid

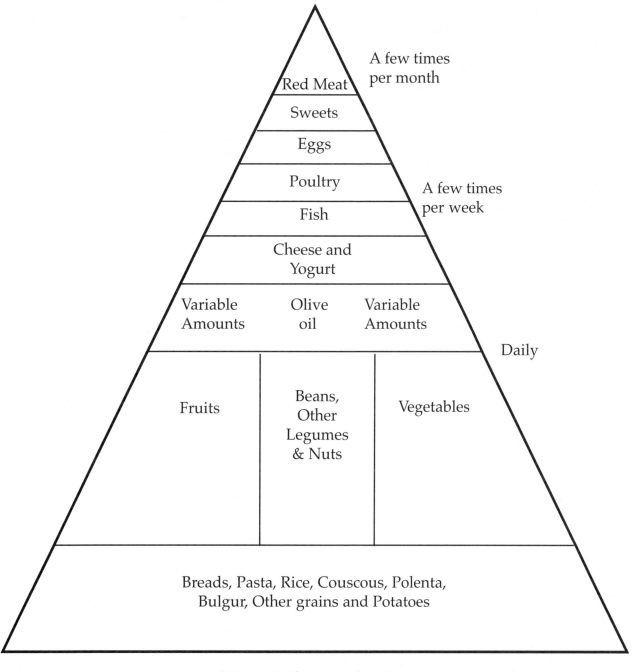

Wine - Daily in moderation

The Mediterranean Pyramid

The last decade has seen a lot of publicity given to the Mediterranean style of eating and has resulted in a pictorial representation known as the Mediterranean Pyramid.

Researchers have documented the longevity and lower incidence of cardiac diseases and diet related cancers among native peoples of the Mediterranean basin. Their diet, which differs substantially from that of most North Americans, notably in the consumption of red meats, saturated fats and refined sugars, is based on the wide use of whole grains, rice, couscous, fruits, vegetables, olives and olive oil.

Wine in moderation is also a key element in this diet.

Nutrition In The Kitchen

For chefs and cooks, understanding nutrition has its logical conclusion when it is taken into the kitchen and is passed on to the customer. Increasingly, restaurant customers are looking for dishes that are more healthful, lower in fat, cholesterol and sodium; yet retain the flavour and freshness that they expect from the best of ingredients.

Observing a few rudimentary guidelines will help you operate a more nutrition friendly kitchen and treat your customers to the style of food they seek.

TIPS FOR A NUTRITION FRIENDLY KITCHEN

1. Design menus that feature at least two appetizers which have reduced fat or no fat calories. Add to this at least two main course items and two desserts that are again, low fat. Dessert could be as simple as a fresh fruit selection.
2. Base some menu items on the highest quality, freshest, local fruit, vegetables, whole grains, nuts and legumes. Not all menu items have to have meat as the centre of attraction.
3. An ideal way to achieve interesting menu items is to explore "fusion" cuisine; a combination of compatible dishes and ideas from different cultures using healthful combinations of whole grains, fruits and vegetables. In the last decade we have seen highly successful "Tex-Mex" and "Cal-Ital". The very popular cuisine of Thailand has established itself in Canada and is now finding its way into our restaurants married to Canadian cuisine.
4. Reducing fat in an established recipe is bound to reduce flavour somewhat since fat carries flavour. To compensate for this flavour loss, experiment with different spices, herbs and condiments added to the dish. Remember, fat is not the only flavour carrier.
5. Cook all foods to maximize flavour and nutrient retention. Steaming is quick and leaches fewer nutrients from foods. Baking requires very little or no added fat to complete cooking.
6. Use non-stick pans to reduce the amount of fat required to saute or pan fry. Remember, every gram of fat has 9 kcalories.
7. Wherever possible use wine, stocks, juices and reductions to substitute for butter, cream and flour and other high calorie, high fat items. Use high calorie foods moderately.
8. Use monounsaturated cooking fats and oils as much as possible, reducing the amount of saturated fats used.
9. Learn the importance of appropriate restaurant portions. When kitchen and serving staff know that dining room portions should not be the same as the dining hall portions in a lumber camp, everyone is further ahead.

10. Consultation with Canadian Heart and Stroke Foundations about "heart-smart" menus and recipes will enable you to achieve your goal of healthier and more nutritional meals.

11. Listen to your guests' menu requests and interests. The success or failure of a menu will rest with them.

Modifying Recipes

Standard recipes do not have to be thrown out to have a healthier dining room menu. The simplest way is to modify recipes you would like to see on the "healthy" list. There are two ways this can be done:
1. by changing the cooking method and,
2. by changing an ingredient(s).

Think more of broiling, roasting, barbecuing or poaching rather than frying. Changing an ingredient is a little more complex since you really have to know what will happen to both taste and in some cases texture of the finished product. Modifying can be done by:
1. reducing an ingredient
2. eliminating the ingredient completely, and
3. substitute with another ingredient.

Reducing an ingredient in baking can be tricky. However, in many cases up to one third of a recipe's sugar can be eliminated without disastrous results.

Eliminating an ingredient entirely requires more thought. Some ingredients may be traditionally necessary to make the dish work, the fat content, for instance, of Pate Cretons of Quebec. However, some less healthy ingredients may be optional, an easier way out.

Substitution can take some experimentation but many are possible and still very flavourful; e.g. low fat yogurt for sour cream, herbs and spices for salt, low fat chicken breast or ground nuts in a meat sauce.

A Little Help From Our Friends

As diligent as we would like to be about selecting the correct products, there is still a lot of confusion to be encountered in the purchasing of packaged food goods. The Canadian Food Inspection Agency comes to the rescue with its governance of packaging and labeling legislation which informs consumers of ingredients, additives, nutritional information, portion sizes and many other pieces of useful information. Reading the label makes you a much more aware consumer.

Study Guide

Summary

- What are some of the concepts of nutrition?
- You must understand the language of nutrition to understand the references in texts, recipes and packaging information.
- Understanding the definition of kcalorie will enable you to select foods and dishes that are most suited to your style of eating.
- Knowing the kcalorie count of different foods will help you regulate your own caloric intake.
- One gram of fat has more than twice the number of kcalories of one gram of carbo hydrate or protein.
- Vitamins, minerals and trace elements are as much a necessity in our diet as are carbohydrate, protein and fat.

WHY IS NUTRITION IMPORTANT?

- Proper nutrition is a guide to healthy living.
- Sound nutritional practices enable one to select recipes and materials consistent with an eating style.
- Cooks and chefs who are aware of proper nutrition are more likely to run a nutrition-friendly kitchen.
- Nutritionally aware cooks and chefs are better equipped to respond to customer requests for particular dietary considerations.

Terms For Review

Macronutrient	Micronutrient	Fat
Carbohydrate	Protein	Fibre
Mineral	Trace element	
Vitamin	Kcalorie	Energy
Saturated fat	Mediterranean pyramid	

Self Assessment Questions

Selected response questions—True or False

1. The science of nutrition carefully outlines what foods you should eat. T F
2. Calorie and kcalorie represent the same amount of energy. T F
3. Carbohydrate, protein and fat are all macronutrients. T F
4. Refined sugar is known as empty calories. T F
5. Dietary fibre is essential to healthy digestion. T F
6. Vitamin A is necessary for good night vision. T F
7. Vegetarians should be aware that not all vegetable proteins are complete proteins. T F
8. Vitamin C deficiency may result in severe tissue damage, particularly connective tissue. T F
9. The Canada Food Guide dictates how many portions of food you should eat daily. T F
10. The essential thing to remember in a daily selection of foods is that balance is as important as quantity. T F

Constructed Short Response Questions

1. Name the four macronutrients.
2. Name the macronutrient that is composed of twenty amino acids.
3. Describe the difference between a low-quality and a high-quality protein.
4. Describe the importance of a sufficient intake of fluoride in the body.
5. Describe a menu that has consideration for guests that prefer low-fat dishes.

Resources and Directory

Fremes/Sabry, 1989, *Nutriscore*, Stoddart Publishing Co.

Whitney, Hamilton, Rolfes, 1995, *Understanding Nutrition*, West Publishing Co.

Drummond, 1989, *Nutrition for the Food Service Professional*, Van Nostrand Reinhold

Garrison, Somer, 1997, *Nutrition Desk Reference*, Keats Publishing

Blonder, 1990, *For Goodness' Sake*, Camden House Lindsay, 1996, *Smart Cooking*, MacMillan Canada

Levy, Dignan, Shirreffs, 1992, *Life & Health*, McGraw-Hill

Fisher, 1995, *Healthy Indulgences*, Hearst Books

Meat Inspection and Grading In Canada

by Larry DeVries

2

Learning Guide

Goal: The purpose of this module is to provide an overview of the
Canadian Meat Inspection and Grading system.

Learning Outcome: After completing this module, you will be able to explain the reasons for meat
inspection and describe the grading systems for beef, pork, veal and lamb.

Learning Objectives: As you work through this module, you will learn to:
1. Explain how Canadian beef, veal, pork and lamb is raised.
2. Describe how Canadian meat is inspected.
3. Categorize the different grades for beef, veal, pork and lamb.

Beef

HISTORY OF BEEF IN CANADA

Where does our Beef come from?

The history of the beef industry in Canada, particularly in western Canada, can be traced back to when the bison were followed throughout their migrations and hunted. The end of the American civil war in 1865 not only brought peace to the US, but also hunger to the aboriginal people of the North American plains. The vast herds of bison, upon which they so heavily relied, were rapidly eradicated. To help meet the demand for meat, the US contracted cattle producers to push large herds of Texas longhorn cattle north to western Canada. When the bison herds were decimated across the western prairies, cattle were introduced into these grasslands to feed and grow, this marked the beginning of the Canadian ranching industry.

The large expanses of grazing land invited foreign investment and the prairie was quickly stocked. The severe winter of the 1906-07 brought this era to an abrupt end when ranchers lost 70 to 100 percent of their cattle. The prairies then opened up to homesteading. As immigrants homesteaded, most farmers owned only a few head of cattle and horses, kept primarily for work. Energy and money went into the production of wheat rather than beef.

By the end of the 1930's tractor power began to replace animal power. In the years that followed, this resulted in the increased availability of feed grains, particularly barley. During the 1950's, the use of corn silage enabled central and eastern Canadian producers to finish cattle more economically than their western counterparts, whose cattle were still being finished on the range. Improved economic conditions and the ready supply of western calves for finishing enabled a large feedlot industry to develop in eastern Canada. As the demand for beef in the eastern industrial cities grew, so did the cattle herds in the western part of the country. The farmers began to feed cattle in smaller areas and so developed the concept of systematically feeding cattle in lots.

Climate, availability of coarse feed grains and improved marketing and transportation alternatives led to the prominent feedlot industry in the early 1970's. The practice of cattle feeding has been an important part of the cattle industry throughout the years. It evolved from this early and simple strategy of allowing cattle to roam and graze on seemingly endless grasslands, to state of the art modern industry, with custom feedlots which use the latest machines, techniques and scientific research.

What Makes Canadian Beef Different?

The Canadian beef industry is an open market and has no marketing boards to manage supplies and marketing. Each sector must function on its own and account for its own profits and losses.

The producer raises the animal from birth until it weighs approximately 300 kg to 350 kg. The beef is then finished (fed a grain ration during the last part of the growing period usually at the 12 - 20 week mark) by the producer or sold to a feedlot operator who will finish the beef. After this stage the animal will be sent to market. Most cattle are sold to processors at the age of about 18 months or a weight of 400 kg to 700 kg. The processor then slaughters the beef and turns it into a hanging carcass. The carcass is then cut into sides or quarters, but most likely processed into boxed beef products. The next step is to either further process the meat or sell it to distributors or directly to food service operators.

Several factors in Canadian beef production makes Canadian beef the most desirable beef in food production around the globe. Modern beef production in Canada uses many years of research, development and marketing to bring the best beef possible to the world market. When cattle are taken off the grasslands and no longer have to roam to feed, the beef is more tender as the animal no longer exercises muscles, which become tough and stronger in flavour the more they are used. Cattle in Canadian feedlots are fed cereal grains that affect the flavour of the meat. Beef in other parts of the world are feed on wild grasses or other types of feed that give a distinctive flavor. Cereal grains give a mild pleasant flavour that is favoured by the North American palate. Development in breeding techniques also have given us a beef that is tender and tasty. Through resourcefulness, hard work and ingenuity from start to finish, Canadian beef is the most desired in the world.

BEEF INSPECTION

Health Inspection

The federal government inspects all meat that is sold across provincial and national boundaries to ensure that is safe and wholesome for human consumption. The consumer can be sure of this, by looking for the health inspection stamp indicates that the meat item purchased meets the federal standards for food safety. Health inspection is not the same as grading and is no indication of the measure of the food quality. This stamp must also appear on meat items entering Canada from other countries.

Inspection is performed by a trained inspector and/or veterinarian who examines every animal before and after slaughter. All inspected carcasses are randomly tested for antibiotics, pesticides, hormones and industrial pollutants.

All substances used for vaccination and medication of livestock must be throughly tested by the Bureau of Veterinary Drugs and Health and Welfare Canada before they are licensed for use.

All livestock arriving at a federally registered establishment must receive a health inspection within 24 hours prior to slaughter. This inspection involves two steps; an initial screening of all animals by an inspector to identify and segregate any suspected of being diseased or in unsatisfactory condition for slaughter, and mandatory veterinary examination and diagnosis of all segregated animals.

After healthy animals are slaughtered, by law all carcasses must undergo postmortem

inspection . This includes an examination of the lymph nodes and internal organs. Any carcass showing signs of significant disease is condemned and sent to an inedible rendering establishment under Agriculture and Agri-Food Canada's control. Only about 0.5% of all red meat carcasses are found not to be fit for human consumption.

Once the inspector passes the meat to be fit and safe for human consumption the inspection seal is stamped into the carcass with a vegetable dye ink. This stamp must also be present on the meat or packaging as it is further processed.

These rigid inspections, tests and controls applied to meat in Canada ensure that only wholesome and disease free meat is sold to Canadian and foreign customers.

Health Inspection Stamp

Healthy Livestock Production

The Health of Animals Act regulates the treatment of cattle from birth to processing. The success of the Canadian cattle industry is dependant on animals being treated in a humane manner. In order to ensure this Canadian producers have developed a Code of Practice for the humane handling of livestock.

In Canada, producers often use livestock medication and vaccination products to make sure their animals are healthy. When cattle become ill, they are treated with antibiotics. Before the livestock is marketed, the producer must observe withdrawal times.

Provincial and Federal Grading

The Canadian beef grading system began in 1929. Many changes have been made since then, and now the system is regarded as on of the best in the world. The Canadian beef grading program compliments Canada's meat inspection program, to form an effective combination for the marketing of Canadian beef.

The system of grading used in Canadian beef divides cattle carcasses into uniform groups to facilitate marketing. This grading system provides an effective way of describing beef so that it is easily understood by both buyers and sellers. Grading provides a system for a buyer to specify a particular grade and a producer to be paid accordingly. In 1992, major changes were made to the grading system to more accurately assess beef quality and yield.

In Canada the grading system is voluntary and is provided through the Canadian Beef Grading Agency in abattoirs that receive either federal or provincial government meat inspection services.

Safe Beef Handling

Beef is marketed in many forms and degrees of processes. The beef may be sold in sides, quarters, primal or as pre-cut and portions. These meats may be sold in either fresh or frozen form.

Most beef is now vacuum sealed packed. A tough, flexible and durable plastic packing film keeps oxygen from coming into contact with the surface of the meat. This slows down the action of spoilage bacteria and the natural tenderizing work of the enzymes in the muscle continues without oxygen. If this packaging loses its seal or leaks, it should be used as soon as possible or returned to the supplier.

Because of a lack of oxygen, packaged beef is a deep purple colour. However, when the beef is exposed to oxygen after the package is opened, the familiar red colour will reappear in 15 to 30 minutes. When vacuumed beef is first opened it will have a slight off odour. The odour comes from the lactic acid bacteria which dominate when oxygen is not present. The odour will

disappear after 15 to 20 minutes exposure to the air. Vacuumed beef will also have a purplish-red fluid inside the bag. This is known as purge or weep. Purge increases over time and excessive purge is a warning sign of temperature abuse or some other problem.

While vacuumed beef has a longer shelf life, it is still subject to spoilage and must be refrigerated or frozen. Vacuumed packaged meat may be keep in the refrigerator for 16 days or more depending on the age of the product when it is received. When opened, vacuumed beef should be used within two days.

To ensure that beef is safe it must be kept cold, clean and covered. That means that all meat should be refrigerated and that surfaces that are in contact with beef should be sanitized and covered to avoid cross-contamination.

QUALITY BEEF GRADES

Quality Grade Criteria

The grade and yield of a carcass determines its value and appropriate use in the food industry. Grading describes the beef eating quality and yield assessment describes the proportion of lean meat in the carcass.

Most Canadian beef is graded, but ungraded beef (mainly imported) is also available. Ungraded beef is inspected for safety and wholesomeness, but its meat quality will be variable.

Canada's top grades have the following common criteria: Meat should be a bright red colour; muscle must be firm and fine grained with good to excellent muscling; external fat covering must be white and firm. The meat should come from youthful animals and minium marbling levels are regulated.

Carcasses are evaluated as either "youthful"or " mature" according to the degree of bone ossification. Youthful carcasses will have a cartilaginous caps on the thoracic vertebrae that are no more than half ossified, and the lumbar vertebrae will show evidence of cartilage or at least as red line presents on the tips.

Youthful carcasses are produced from cattle generally less than 24 months of age, but would be no more than 30 months of age. Carcasses showing more advanced ossification are considered to be mature and must be graded in one of the Canada D grades or as in the case of a bull, Canada E.

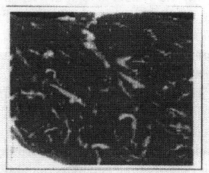

MINIMUM REQUIREMENT IS SLIGHTLY ABUNDANT MARBLING

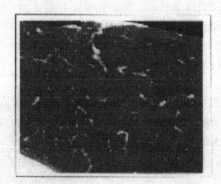

MINIMUM REQUIREMENT IS SMALL MARBLING

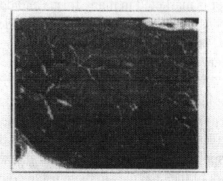

MINIMUM REQUIREMENT IS SLIGHT MARBLING

MINIMUM REQUIREMENT IS TRACE MARBLING (NOT DEVOID)

Grade Names

Canada Grade A/AA/AAA/Prime Grades

There are 13 beef grades in the Canadian system. They are:
Canada A, Canada AA, Canada AAA,
Canada Prime
Canada B1, Canada B2, Canada B3,
Canada B4
Canada D1, Canada D2, Canada D3,
Canada D4
Canada E

The difference between the three "A" grades - AAA, AA, and A, relates to the amount of marbling, or fine white streaks of fat running through the lean meat. AAA is the most marbled and has the best overall eating quality. Marbling contributes to tenderness, taste, and juiciness, therefore resulting in a more consistent product.

The four highest grades (Prime, A, AA, AAA) represent almost 89% of all graded Canadian beef carcasses. The grade criteria for these four grades are identical, with the only exception being degrees of marbling.

Carcasses must be youthful to be graded in these grades. This ensures a high level of tenderness in all three grades of high quality Canadian beef. Muscling must range from good with no deficiencies, to excellent. The ribeye muscle must have a bright red colour and be firm in texture. There is a minium external fat thickness of 4 mm required at the ribeye measurement site, and the external fat must be firm and white, or no more than slightly tinged with reddish or amber colour.

To distinguish between A, AA, AAA and Prime graded carcasses, the grader evaluates the level of marbling:

- A carcass with a minium of trace marbling, youthful characteristics, bright red colour, and white fat will be designated with **CANADA -A** grade.
- A carcass with similar characteristics but with a minium of slight marbling will be designated with a **CANADA - AA** grade.

- A carcass with similar high quality characteristics but with a minium of small marbling will be designated **CANADA - AAA** grade.
- A carcass , again with similar high quality characteristics but with a minium of slightly abundant marbling will be designated **CANADA PRIME**.

Red ink is used for A's and Prime grades.

Canada B Grades

Canada B grades are youthful animals.

B1 No marbling *Less than 4 mm exterior fat*
B2 Yellow fat
B3 Poor Muscling
B4 Dark meat colour
Blue ink is used for B grades.

Canada D and E Grades

D and E grades are mature, older animals. Mature older animals that are used primarily for ground beef or processed products such as sausages and lunch meats. These carcasses are usually not graded and are marketed as ungraded product.
Brown ink is used for D grades. Question

Yield Grades

In Canada, all A/AA/AAA/Prime graded carcasses must also be graded for the lean meat yield content in the carcass. This differs from the United States where quality and yield grading are coupled, and consequently there is no guarantee that both quality and yield assessments will be made of individual carcasses.

Canadian cattle producers wish to encourage a system where producers receive a higher payment for animals which yield more meat for each high quality grade.

There are three possible yield grades in the Canadian system:
1. Carcasses exhibiting high quality characteristics and are estimated to

contain 59% or more lean meat are designated yield classification **CANADA 1**

2. Carcasses exhibiting the same high quality characteristics and are estimated to contain between 54% and 58% lean meat are designated yield classification **CANADA 2**.

3. Carcasses with high quality characteristics and are estimated to contain 53% or less lean meat are designated yield classification **CANADA 3**.

The yield grades are not determined for any carcass graded in the B, D, or E grades. The carcass meat yield is determined on the basis of carcass weight, ribeye muscle size, and external fat thickness at the ribeye. To enable the grader to estimate the carcass meat yield quickly, a special ruler has been developed by Agriculture and Agri-Food Canada.

Ground beef is the most popular form of beef eaten in Canada. The fat content varies in different forms of ground beef. Federal government labeling regulations require that ground beef be labeled as:

Extra lean - maximum fat content 10%
Lean   - maximum fat content 17%
Medium   - maximum fat content 23%
Regular   - maximum fat content 30%

The fat percentages are regulated by law and government inspectors regularly check samples to ensure meat is labeled correctly.

Boxed Beef Grading

Beef improves with age. The term aging simply means the length of time beef cuts are stored under controlled temperature and humidity conditions before they are packed. Aging allows naturally occurring enzymes within the meat to slowly break down some of the connective tissues that contribute to toughness.

Beef aging significantly increases tenderness. Aging times vary considerably from 3-21 days. For best eating quality beef should be aged at least 10 -14 days.

This ageing takes place on carcass beef. The Canadian beef exporting industry has largely moved away from sales of carcass beef, toward sale of boxed beef. Boxed beef is not aged on the carcass, but rather, in heavy sealed plastic bags. One danger in moving into a boxed beef program is the potential loss of grade identity for a particular carcass.

All Canadian boxed beef product distributed domestically or exported by federally inspected Canadian establishments must carry a grade identity. This identification system is monitored closely by Agriculture and Agri-Food Canada government employees. The key benefit to this program is the absolute assurance on the part of the buyer that the product within the box bears the grade for the carcass from which it was derived.

Comparisons to the U.S.D.A. Grading System

The Canadian beef grading system was changed substantially in 1992 to include marbling standards developed in Canada that were based on the same criteria as those used in the United States in terms of size, distribution, and number of marbling particles. The number of marbling categories used, however, is different between the two countries. The United States has four primary quality grades for youthful carcasses, which are Prime, Choice, Select, and Standard. Marbling requirements for the Canada Prime, AAA and AA grades are essentially the same as for the U.S.D.A. Prime, Choice and Select grades respectively. Canada A is unique to Canada, in that it possesses all high quality attributes and trace marbling levels.

To establish the degree of similarity in assignment of beef quality grades in the U.S.A. and Canada, two studies were conducted in 1994 on over 4,600 carcasses in the two countries. The studies were conducted by the National Grade Standards Officers of both countries who assessed each of the 4,600 carcasses independently and assigned a final quality grade to the carcass. This study showed that there is a high degree association (approximately 85%) between the marbling standards of the Canadian and American high quality beef grades. It is important to note that the USDA Standard grade may be practically devoid of marbling, therefore making any association between this grade and a Canadian beef grade inappropriate.

Although there is a high degree of association between the top quality Canadian and American grades, the grade criteria other than marbling are stricter for the Canada A, AA, AAA and Prime grades. The Canadian grading system allows no "quality attribute offsets."

The American system will allow carcasses from animals up to 42 months of age (B age category) to stay in their Prime, Choice and Standard grades if the carcasses show higher levels of marbling. The Canadian grading system will automatically remove all mature animals (over 30 months of age based on physiological criteria) from the four high quality grades (A/AA/AAA/Prime) to either the "D" or "E" grades.

The American system will penalize black cutter (black colour) beef by no more than one full grade (i.e., Prime to Choice, Choice to Select or Select to Standard). Dark cutter (dark colour) beef will be discounted by less than one full grade (i.e., High Choice to Low Choice). It is, therefore, possible for dark coloured beef to be graded Choice, Select or Standard in the United States. The Canadian grading system will automatically remove all dark cutter beef from the four high quality grades (A/AA/AAA/Prime) to the B4 grade.

The American system also does not recognize yellow fat as a quality discount factor. The Canadian grading system will automatically remove all carcasses with yellow fat from the four high quality grades.

Canada has successfully reduced problems associated with all drug residues through the use of such extensive programs. For example, the level of compliance for pesticide residues over the past five years has been over 99.65 and the presence of antibiotics in beef and veal is an extremely rare occurrence. The high degree of achievement is, however, not taken for granted. Government managers of the Canadian meat inspection program are always planning

strategies for the future.

Through Agriculture and Agri-Food Canada's export program, government officials work to develop and increase the favourable export trade for Canadian produced beef and veal products by ensuring that import standards of foreign countries are met by the Canadian meat inspection system. Industry and abattoir government inspection staff are kept up-to-date with changing requirements of importing countries with the help of a reference book which lists all such requirements. Detailed requirements of foreign countries are also available to inspection staff on the federal government's national computerized AgriNet database system. This links all regional offices allowing inspectors to refer quickly and efficiently to this export information. Information from over 100 meat importing nations is listed. Aspects of the export program are reviewed and negotiated with representative of foreign governments with a view to their effect on domestic and international market development. Procedures are developed for the Canadian meat inspection service to meet the import requirements of foreign countries.

Bacterial contamination during processing is of major concern to the federal government inspection service. Muscle tissue of healthy animals is normally free of bacteria. Contamination may occur during slaughter and subsequent processing. Spoilage organisms and pathogens from the environment and the animal's intestinal tract are the primary sources of bacterial contamination. The federal government Bacterial Monitoring Program monitors meat products at critical stages of production to verify that the establishment's processing methods and quality control measures are adequate to assure safe and uncontaminated meat products.

Canada's meat inspection service is shifting efforts from detection to prevention as it is transformed from a reactive to proactive service that seeks to identify and eliminate potential threats to food safety and wholesomeness before they become problems. It seeks to focus efforts on the "invisible" threats to safety — the twin problems of residues and bacterial contamination. The development and implementation of rapid tests that can be conducted at the abattoir level are part of this federal government priority. The use of such screening tests has many advantages. First of all, it drastically decreases costs, as only presumptive positive samples will be forwarded to regional laboratories for further analysis, allowing for many more tests to be completed. Secondly, the majority of these tests provide results within hours, allowing for quick response to potential health risks. Thirdly, they provide government inspectors with a more scientific means to carry out their duties.

Detection and control programs for salmonella, listeria and other food pathogens represent a very high priority. The detection of all other residues will also continue to be a priority. Our government and industry residue and pathogen detection program continues to grow to provide Canadian and international consumers of Canadian meat with a safe and wholesome product. These advances are consistent with the Hazard Analysis Critical Control Points (HACCP) preventative system of food safety control that was developed with companies supplying food for the U.S. space flights. All federally inspected meat processing establishments will be required by the Government of Canada to incorporate comprehensive HACCP programs in the very near future — many have already done so.

All export shipments of meat products from Canada must originate from federally registered and inspected establishments. In all cases, exports of Canadian meat from any Canadian abattoir must be accompanied by an Agriculture and Agri-Food Canada inspection certificate. This certificate can only be signed by a federal government veterinarian. Each package of the shipment must be identified with either an export stamp bearing the certificate number or with an export sticker whose serial number is listed on the certificate. These stickers and stamps are kept under tight security by on-site government inspectors. This mandatory requirement assures

that all meat exported from Canada has been processed in a federally inspected abattoir, and that the abattoir has complied with all inspection requirements. This is our seal of food safety.

Aspects of the export program are reviewed and negotiated with representatives of foreign governments with a view to their effect on domestic and international market development. Procedures are developed for the Canadian government inspection service to meet import requirements of foreign countries.

The Government of Canada (Agriculture and Agri-Foods Canada), in consultation with the Canadian beef industry, is constantly reviewing regulations to ensure that the safety and marketability of Canadian beef is maintained and improved. A consultation mechanism is in place which permits input from all sectors of the industry with regard to concerns about the inspection systems. In addition, specific export needs for importing countries can be accommodated by the Canadian beef inspection program.

Veal

Generally speaking veal is a male dairy calf. Only a select few of these calves are used in the dairy industry for breeding, the rest are raised as veal calves.

There are two types of veal, grain-fed and milk-fed veal. Grain-fed veal is pink in colour. The calf is fed a milk based diet only for the first 6-8 weeks. During this time grains are also gradually introduced into the diet. The calf is then raised to between 270-300 kg. Milk-fed veal is light pink in colour and fed a balanced liquid diet. The calf is marketed at about 200 kg.

Veal calves are raised in barns that are well lit, insulated, and ventilated. At one time it was believed that veal raised in an environment void of light produced a lighter fleshed meat. However, the absence of light has no effect on the colour or the quality of the meat. Individual stalls are proven to meet the needs of the calf with the least amount of stress. The calf can lie down, stand up, groom itself, and have social contact. The stalls are designed so the calf does not have to be tied. Exercise has no effect on the tenderness or quality of the meat.

Veal calves are fed a balanced diet with added energy, vitamins, and minerals, including iron. Veal feeds do not contain antibiotics unless prescribed by a veterinarian because a calf is ill. All animal medications in Canada are approved by Agriculture and Agri-Food Canada and the bureau of Veterinary Drugs.

Every animal must be inspected before and after processing in a licensed meat processing plants. All meat plants are inspected by Provincial or Federal government veterinarians. Guidelines for raising veal calves are set out in the " Recommended Code of Practice for the Care and Handling of Milk-Fed Veal Calves". Veal farming has created a quality food product from a by-product of the dairy industry in Canada.

VEAL IN CANADIAN CUISINE

The veal industry in Canada developed as a result of European immigration and thus, influences in our cuisine. As these chefs were accustomed to using veal in their cooking, so the demand for Canadian veal grew. Most veal in Canada is grown and used in the eastern provinces. Veal is becoming a more popular meat in the retail and resturant trade.

The term Provimi veal in Canada was a marketing tool so that veal product sounded more European. The word Provimi is simply the first letters of the words protein, vitamin, and mineral.

VEAL INSPECTION

Veal inspection follows the same criteria as for beef inspection. All veal must be slaughtered at registered establishments where an inspector will inspect the live animal as well as the carcass after slaughter. The inspection assures the consumer that the veal is healthy and fit for human consumption.

VEAL GRADES

Youthful veal carcasses, weighing less than 150 kg (hide off) are classified as veal within the Canadian beef grading program. Veal carcasses are graded for quality on the basis of meat colour, overall muscling, and fat cover.

Veal carcasses with at least good muscling and some creamy white fat are graded CANADA - A. Those with low to medium muscling and excess of a fat are graded CANADA - B. Veal carcasses failing to meet the requirements of CANADA - B are graded CANADA - C.

All veal carcasses are then graded for meat colour. The veal grader uses a colour reflectance meter to do this. The carcasses are assigned a numerical value based on the objective measurement of meat colour. Veal carcasses are segregated into four colour classifications, based on meter reading values. As meat colour becomes more pink, grades of 2, 3, and 4 are assigned. As muscle and back fat quality decreases, muscling scores will move to 2, 3, or 4. The lowest quality of Canadian veal is therefore produced from carcasses grading C4. This process of muscle and colour grading ensures that purchasers of Canadian veal can specific their exact quality requirements.

Pork

The majority of Canadian hogs are raised indoors under climatically controlled conditions. Today's barns use sophisticated ventilation and heating systems to regulate air temperature, relative humidity, airflow patterns, and levels of dust and gas. Climate control is key to swine comfort, health and reproductive efficiency in today's barns. Swine feed must also meet equally high standards for nutritional value and hygiene.

Access to barns is rigidly controlled to keep animal free of disease. Barn workers routinely shower and change into clean overall before entering the barn to maintain high health standards. Manure is also closely managed. It is regularly flushed out of the barn and stored into holding tanks or lagoons until it can be recycled on the fields as fertilizer.

PORK MARKETING IN CANADA

Farmers that produce hogs work independently from one another, but work together through their provincial hog marketing boards to bring about the orderly and effective marketing of their hogs. These marketing boards are responsible for the sale of market hogs in their province and are under the exclusive and direct control of hog producers, but do not regulate supply.

The market is based on supply and demand and is fast and efficient, with electronic sales systems where hogs are sold in lots. A lot of hogs (200) can be sold in approximately 30 seconds. Producers receive their payments through their marketing board on a dressed carcass weight basis.

Canadian pork is usually offered for sale in the form of primal cuts, consisting of the butt, picnic, belly, loin and leg. It is usually leaner than U.S. pork and the Canadian style of cutting differs slightly from the U.S. particularly in the loin and shoulder cuts.

Approximately 50% of all Canadian pork is further processed into cooked and cured products.

PORK INSPECTION

All pork and pork products that are sold for export and for interprovincial trade must be in slaughtered in a federally registered slaughter or processing establishment that meets the federal standards. Inspection is administered by the Canadian Food Inspection Agency under the Meat Inspection Act.

Depending on the province, meat may or may not be required to be inspected in order to be sold. In some provinces, inspection for slaughtering, and inspection required for retail meat sales may be voluntary. In provinces that require inspection this comes under the administration of the Provincial Departments of Agriculture or Health, and varies from province to province.

Any meat unfit for human consumption is condemned and destroyed, or rendered into nonedible by-products.

PORK GRADES

Canada's carcass classification and settlement system provides a national standard set of weight and leanness categories. This system is mandatory and is carried out on location at each packing establishment. The system classifies carcasses into indexes based on back fat measurement on the split carcass and on warm weight including head, kidney, leaf lard and feet. The purpose of the system is to measure the carcass meat yield content. The system is fair, impartial and objective and encourages production of higher quality pork.

Yield and weight classes focus on leanness and core weight of hogs in the 75 to 90 kg range. This provides incentives to producers to market hogs that fall in that core area, in line with consumer's demand for leaner pork.

Lamb

LAMB PRODUCTION IN CANADA

The growing of sheep and lamb in Canada may of well began with the arrival of European settlers bringing stocks of sheep with them to begin life in a new country over 500 years ago. Traditionally, Canadians have not been large consumers of lamb in comparison to people in other parts of the world. This is more than likely due to our strong beef growing capabilities. Also, during World War II many servicemen serving overseas, were often fed rations of a much stronger flavoured mutton. However, the consumption of lamb in Canada is on the rise as consumers are discovering the fine flavour of lamb.

The majority of Canadian sheep producers raise market lambs, which are later fed to produce meat for the consumer's plate. Most often a crossbred ewe is bred to a purebred ram, and all lambs are marketed as commercial lamb. Ewes are bred to lamb between January and May, with top dollar going to those lambs which reach market earliest. Out-of-season breeding with appropriate breeds means lambs are produced year-round, providing a more consistent supply for the market place. The degree of success depends on feeding and management.

Lambs weighing 20 to 35 kg are placed into a dry lot and fed hay, grain and supplements to a targeted weight of 45 to 50 kg when they are marketed as butcher lambs. A variety of sheep and lambs are sold at local auction barns, while some are purchased by stock buyers on-farm. Finished lamb carcasses are sold at farm-gate to private customers, making up a potion of domestic lamb consumption.

LAMB INSPECTION

Lamb that is to be sold commercially must be slaughtered in an approved killing plant that meets all the regulations as set out by the Canadian Food Inspection Agency. Lamb sold in Canada must have the Health Inspection Stamp on the Carcass or container. This ensures that the lamb is wholesome and safe for human consumption.

LAMB GRADES

While inspection is mandatory for the slaughter of lamb, grading is voluntary, and is not required in order to be sold. There is a grading system for lamb that determines the quality of the meat. Grade A and Grade B lamb is sold to commercial and retail outlets. The criteria for these grades is based on the amount of fat in ratio to lean, colour of lean, and amount of surface fat. However, much of the lamb sold in Canada, is ungraded.

Study Guide

Terms for Review

Inspection	Grading	Carcass
Boxed Beef	Marbling	Aging
Veal	Provimi	Muscle

Canadian Food Inspection Agency
Health Inspection Stamp

Questions for Discussion

1. What are 3 factors that makes Canadian Beef more desirable to the Canadian Palate?
2. Why is meat inspection a critical part of food production?
3. How can we be sure that the meat we consume has been inspected?
4. Why has vacuumed sealed beef become the most common way of selling beef ?
5. What are the thirteen Grades of Canadian Beef and what does the grade mean?
6. What are four factors that distinguish Canadian Beef from American Beef ?
7. What are three differences between milk-fed and grain-fed veal ?

Acknowledgements

Agriculture and Agri-Food
Alberta Cattle Feeders' Association
Beef Information Centre
Canada Beef Export Federation
Canadian Food Inspection Agency
Canada Pork International
Manitoba Agriculture
Manitoba Pork
Ontario Veal association
Saskatchewan Agriculture and Food
The Ontario Sheep Marketing Agency

Poultry and Egg Inspection and Grading In Canada

by Andrew Ormiston

3

What's In It For Us

- Do you want to have a better understanding of poultry and egg inspection and grading in Canada?
- Do you want to be able to determine whether the poultry and eggs you use have been inspected and graded?
- Do you want to know what the benefits of poultry and egg inspection are?
- Do you want to be able to choose the most appropriate grade of poultry or eggs for the needs of your kitchen?

This module will provide you with an introduction to the systems of inspection and grading of poultry and eggs in Canada. It is a common misconception that all the foods we purchase and use in our kitchens have been rigorously checked by government inspectors for disease and contamination. In fact in some parts of Canada, no inspection is required at all for some food items. You will also learn that some of the foods you use most commonly may not have been graded. Considering the current litigation climate in this country, it is wise for all of us involved in the food services to be aware of any shortcomings or weaknesses in our local, provincial or federal food inspection systems.

Learning Guide

Goal: The purpose of this module is to provide an overview of the inspection and grading of poultry and eggs in Canada.

Learning Outcome: After completing this module you will be able to describe what inspection and grading are and identify the various grades and kinds of poultry and eggs available to you.

Learning Objectives: After you work through this module you will be able to:
1. Describe what "Inspection" means–discuss the systems of inspection and the agencies involved in poultry and egg inspection in Canada and decide whether our current systems are appropriate for us in the 21st century.
2. Determine whether the poultry and eggs you use have been inspected and by whom by being able to identify inspection legends.
3. Describe what "Grading" means and be able to identify the various grades of eggs and poultry - by being able to read grading logos so that you can choose the most appropriate grade for your needs.

Prerequisite: You should have a basic understanding of sanitation and the bacteria which are most commonly associated with poultry and eggs.

Meat Inspection In Canada

Meat inspection is a major part of Canada's food inspection system. Its purpose is to ensure consumers a safe supply of wholesome meat products and to help Canadian meat producers and processors gain access to international markets.

Meat is inspected in Canada within an environment involving federal, provincial and municipal jurisdiction. This has led to overlapping responsibilities, legislative and regulatory burdens for producers, processors and shippers, and increased impediments to interprovincial and international trade.

The Canadian Food Inspection Implementation Group is examining the possibilities of developing a national meat code in order to harmonize federal and provincial standards governing the production and processing of meat products. At present, meat inspection activities operate under several models in Canada.

FEDERAL INSPECTION

- is available to any federally registered slaughter or processing facility.

- is mandatory for meat processors who wish to export their products interprovincially or internationally.

- is provided by the Canadian Food Inspection Agency (CFIA) under the Meat Inspection Act.

- consists of pre-slaughter inspection, postmortem inspection of carcasses, chemical residue monitoring, and inspection of all processing and storage operations. Slaughter and inspection activities are under veterinary supervision.

FEDERAL

- is provided by CFIA staff on behalf of the provinces of British Columbia, Saskatchewan and Manitoba.

- allows meat processors to trade only within their respective provinces.

PROVINCIAL INSPECTION

- is not mandatory in all provinces, thus many smaller establishments are not inspected at all.

- allows a meat processor to trade its products only within its province.

- is usually provided by the respective provincial Department of Agriculture or Health.

Construction, operating standards and types of inspection vary from province to province. There are major discrepancies among the provinces in the way slaughter and processing establishments are inspected and regulated. Not all provinces require pre-slaughter inspection, veterinary supervision or inspection of processing and storage operations. Provincial standards are generally not as stringent as federal in regard to physical plant facilities.

ADOPTION OF A NATIONAL MEAT INSPECTION STANDARD

Changing market forces, evolving international standards, technical advances, increasing public expectations and fiscal realities are pressuring federal and provincial authorities to adopt a single, internationally accepted standard for the inspection of food in this country. Canada's trade aspirations and internal and external trade agreements (AIT, GATT, NAFTA, CUSTA) mean there are now, or soon will be, specific requirements for food inspection in this country. For example, Canadian food processors wishing to export to the USA must meet USDA Pathogen Reduction and HAACP Rules.

The Canadian Food Inspection Agency (CFIA) and some provincial governments are responding to these challenges by implementing HAACP (Hazard Analysis Critical Control Points) based inspection systems. HAACP is an internationally recognized, scientifically-based method of assessing food hazards and has been adopted by a number of countries.

Under the present interpretation of our internal and external trade agreements, foods imported into Canada must meet federal standards for food safety. However, there are differing legal opinions on the validity of this position. Without a single, enforced national standard, imported foods would probably flow through the province with the least stringent food safety requirements and controls would need to be implemented to ensure that the product remained within that province or territory. This is creating pressure for the provinces to harmonize their standards as such controls would contradict federal-provincial initiatives to eliminate interprovincial trade barriers.

In 1994 a National Domestic Standard was developed for meat slaughter, process-
ing and inspection. Unfortunately the standard was not adopted because some provinces regarded it as more stringent than necessary. It was also unclear what impact a single, national standard would have on small businesses.

Further work on the proposed standard is being performed by a joint committee of federal, provincial, territorial and municipal representatives from Agriculture, Fisheries and Health Agencies who see a need for a comprehensive system of food inspection in Canada. Their goals are a high quality, safe food supply, harmonized standards, risk based inspection systems, cost reduction, protection from economic fraud and enhanced access to markets for Canadian food producers. *(Canadian Food Inspection System Implementation Group background paper)*

The Canadian Food Inspection Agency

The government of Canada has recently consolidated all federal food inspection and quarantine services into a single federal food inspection agency. The Canadian Food Inspection Agency (CFIA) began operations in April 1997 as an agency of Agriculture and Agri-Food Canada.

Formerly the delivery of federal inspection, grading and quarantine services was delivered by elements of Agriculture and Agri-Food Canada, Health Canada, Industry Canada and the Department of Fisheries and Oceans Canada. All federal inspection services related to food safety are now provided by the CFIA. Health Canada retains responsibility for food safety policy, standard-setting, risk assessment and analytical testing research. They set the federal standards for food safety in Canada: the CFIA enforces those standards.

The CFIA is a federal government initiative and has jurisdiction over food which will trade interprovincially or will be exported. The Agency also has authority over food imports. The provinces and some municipalities retain varying levels of jurisdiction over foods which will not leave their respective provinces.
(CFIA)

Poultry Inspection and Grading

INSPECTION AND MONITORING OF POULTRY PRODUCTION AND PROCESSING FACILITIES

All poultry processing facilities under federal jurisdiction are registered with the CFIA and must be licensed by the agency to slaughter and process poultry. Any poultry product which will be shipped across provincial boundaries or will be exported must be slaughtered and processed in a licensed establishment. The CFIA sets and enforces the standards which such establishments must meet in regard to building standards, sanitation procedures, food handling and food storage. Under several federal-provincial agreements, the CFIA also performs inspection services in some slaughtering and processing facilities which are under the jurisdiction of their respective provinces.
(CFIA)

INSPECTION OF POULTRY AND POULTRY PRODUCTS BY CFIA

All poultry slaughtered and processed at CFIA licensed facilities is inspected for wholesomeness by CFIA inspectors. CFIA inspection services are constantly evolving to use inspection resources more efficiently and effectively, and to meet the changing needs of the industry. New inspection systems that improve on traditional inspection systems by using Hazard Analysis and Critical Control Point (HACCP) and audit principles have been introduced in certain plants across Canada. These new systems enhance the responsibility of the plant operator for assuring the quality of the product.

Inspection is:

a) A method for verifying that the meat product conforms to regulatory standards and is wholesome.

b) Indicated by a distinctive inspection legend.

c) Required for poultry which will cross provincial boundaries or be exported.

One of these legends, displayed on the wrapper, box or case, indicates that the CFIA has inspected the poultry and found it fit for human consumption.

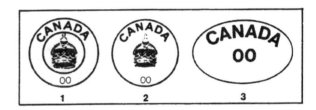

(CFIA - by permission)

Canadian Poultry Grading System

Grading is:

a) An indicator of quality.

b) Indicated by a maple leaf outline with letter grade

c) Not mandatory in Canada.

CANADIAN POULTRY GRADES

Poultry is graded as: Canada A, Canada Utility or Canada C. Canada A and Canada Utility are the most common grades in food service use. Canada C is uncommon and rarely seen. A case or box of poultry, most often seen in food service use, will have one of these grading logos clearly marked on it.

(CFIA - by permission)

A bird which is individually wrapped at the processing plant may have a colored grading logo on its wrapping. This is most often encountered on birds sold on the retail market.

  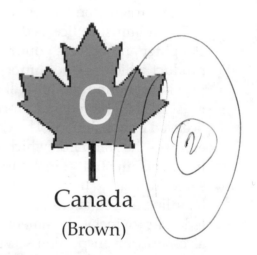

Canada
(Red)

Canada
(Blue)

Canada
(Brown)

(CFIA - by permission)

POULTRY IMPORTED INTO CANADA

Poultry imported into Canada must:

- have been prepared under conditions equivalent to those prescribed by Canada's *Meat Inspection Act and Regulations*.
- have originated in a country that has grade standards equivalent to Canada's.
- meet the standards of one of Canada's poultry grades.
- be clearly labeled as the product of a country other than Canada.

(CFIA)

MAJOR FACTORS IN POULTRY GRADING

Whole birds sold on the retail market or for commercial use are graded on the following criteria: *(see next page)*

Allowed	Canada A	Utility
Tears in Skin	Up to 6 mm in total on the breast if the carcass is under 5.5 kg. 2.5 cm in total elsewhere. Up to 1.2 cm in total on the breast if the carcass is over 5.5 kg. 3.5 cm in total elsewhere.	Skin missing on up to $^1/_2$ the breast area.
Missing Parts	Wing tips, tail. Ducks and geese may also be missing the flat wings	Wings, one entire leg or both drum sticks. The tail may be removed and small areas of flesh may be missing.
Skeleton	Keel may be slightly crooked.	Keel may be slightly crooked.
Discoloration of Flesh	Up to 1.6 cm^2 in total on the breast. Up to 6.5 cm^2 in total elsewhere on the carcass.	Up to 6.5 cm^2 in total on the breast. Up to 8 cm^2 in total elsewhere on the carcass.
Flesh	Breast must be moderately plump.	Breast must not fall away sharply from keel bone.
Fat	Breasts, thighs and back show evidence of fat covering.	Sufficient fat to prevent flesh from appearing clearly.
Broken or Dislocated Bones	None.	Wing & leg bones may be dislocated. No broken bones.

Carcasses graded **Canada C** are normally mature chickens that do not meet the standards for **Canada A** or **Canada Utility**. They may have discolorations of up to 14.5 cm^2 in total on the carcass but must have sufficient flesh on the breast to prevent extremely sharp falling away from the keel bone. They are usually sold to processors.

Since grading of poultry is not mandatory in Canada, widely used products such as chicken wings and boneless, skinless chicken breasts are often from ungraded birds.

(CFIA, Chicken Farmers of Canada)

COMMON CHICKEN AND TURKEY CATEGORIES

Kind	Category	Description	Weight Range
Chicken	Rock Cornish hen	A young chicken, very tender flesh.	Under 900 g.
	Broiler or fryer	Young chicken of either sex. The most commonly produced category of chicken.	900g to 1.6 kg.
	Roaster	A larger and more mature bird.	Greater than 1.6 kg.
	Capon	Desexed male chicken. Large and very tender breast.	Variable.
Turkey	Broiler	Young bird of either sex.	Up to 5 kg.
	Hen	A maturing female bird.	5 to 8 kg.
	Tom	A more mature bird of either sex.	Greater than 8 kg.

(Manitoba Chicken Marketing Board, Manitoba Turkey Producers, Chicken Farmers of Canada, Canadian Turkey Marketing Agency)

DEFINITIONS

Free range: Poultry allowed to roam out of doors, usually in pens. They may or may not be organically raised. Free range poultry will be more expensive than free run or cage-raised birds.

Free run: Poultry allowed to roam in large barns and eat and drink at will, as opposed to birds raised in cages.

Organic: Poultry raised without the use of pesticides or antibiotics. Poultry products which claim to be "organic" or "organically farmed" should bear a label indicating the name or number of the certifying body which carried out the inspection and has certified that the production, processing, packaging and distribution of the product meets the standards for organic certification. Some poultry products may claim to be raised without growth hormones. In fact, all Canadian poultry is raised without them as the use of growth hormones is illegal in this country. Organically raised poultry usually commands a premium price.

(BC Turkey Marketing Agency, CFIA)

EXOTIC BREEDS PRODUCED AND SOLD IN CANADA

This is a developing industry in some parts of Canada.

Ostrich, emu and rhea, collectively known as ratites, are raised for their feathers, hide, eggs, fat and meat. These birds are often slaughtered and processed by beef processors due to their size. A common cutting system has been developed for ratites.

Pheasant, quail, Guinea fowl, partridge, silkie, squab, poussin and wild turkey are now raised in several provinces. As these birds are often raised with the expectation that they will be shipped across provincial boundaries or exported, they are usually inspected, slaughtered and processed at CFIA licensed plants. There is as yet no standard grading system in place for these birds, though some producers and processors have developed private systems and national standards have been requested for Guinea fowl. They may be sold whole, partially boned, boneless or as prepared portions, depending on the supplier and the demands of the market.
(Canadian Ostrich Association, Mark Hills - Hills Foods Ltd., Burnaby, B.C.)

The Canadian Poultry Production and Marketing System

Domestic chicken and turkey are produced and marketed in Canada under a system known as supply management. Under a Federal-Provincial agreement, each provincial marketing organization is assigned an annual quota of chicken and turkey to produce. The quota is determined principally by the Canadian Turkey Marketing Agency and the Chicken Farmers of Canada in consultation with poultry processors and representatives of the retail and food service sectors.

Each provincial marketing organization then assigns quotas to the poultry producers within its province. The effect of supply management has been to ensure reliable supplies, reasonably stable prices to poultry farmers, the viability of smaller producers and, arguably, to maintain higher prices for consumers.
(Chicken Farmers of Canada, Canadian Turkey Marketing Board)

Egg Inspection and Grading

INSPECTION AND MONITORING OF EGG PRODUCTION AND PROCESSING FACILITIES

Eggs destined for interprovincial trade or for export must come from an egg grading station which is registered with the CFIA. The Agency sets and enforces the standards which registered egg grading stations must meet in regard to physical facilities and egg handling, grading, storage procedures and labelling.

INSPECTION OF EGGS AND EGG PRODUCTS

At the grading station eggs are washed, sanitized, graded, weighed and packed. As a part of the regular CFIA inspection, inspectors take random samples of eggs. Samples are assessed to ensure that they meet the requirements of the *Egg Regulations*.

Inspection is:
a) A process to monitor the wholesomeness of eggs.
b) Monitoring to see that the egg meets its grade standards.
c) Required for eggs which will trade interprovincially or be exported.

(CFIA, Canadian Egg Marketing Agency)

CANADIAN EGG GRADING SYSTEM

Grading is:
a) An indicator of quality.
b) Indicated by a letter grade within a maple leaf.
c) Mandatory for all eggs intended for the table market.

CANADIAN EGG GRADES

There are four grades of eggs: Canada A, Canada B, Canada C and Canada Nest Run. Canada A eggs are sold for household or commercial use. Canada B eggs are sold for commercial baking or further processing. Canada C is sold only for further processing. Canada Nest Run eggs may be sold for further processing or sent to another grading station to be regraded.

Only Canada A eggs sold for retail use, and Canada B eggs, sold for commercial use will have their grade clearly indicated on their box or carton.

Major factors in egg grading   *(CFIA - by permission)*

	Canada A	Canada B
Yolk	Must be round and well centred.	Distinct yolk outline, moderately oblong, floats freely. May have a very slight degree of germ development.
Albumen	Reasonably firm.	No requirements.
Air Cell	Not more than 5 mm in depth.	Not more than 9 mm. in depth.
Shell	Is clean, uncracked and has no more than 3 stains which total no more than 25 mm². Must be normal or nearly normal in shape. May have rough areas and moderate ridges.	May have dirt spots of up to a total area of 40 mm² and stains not exceeding 320 mm². Must be uncracked but can be slightly abnormal in shape. May have rough areas and definite ridges.
Weight	See sizing requirements pg. 43	Must weigh at least 49 grams.

(CFIA, Canadian Egg Marketing Agency)

SIZING REQUIREMENTS

Only Canada A eggs are sized under the following criteria: *(see chart below)*

EGGS IMPORTED INTO CANADA

Eggs imported into Canada must:

- have originated in a country that has a system of inspection and grading requirements equivalent to those prescribed in Canada.
- be equivalent to a Canadian grade.
- have the size designation marked on the container if they are Grade A.
- be transported directly to a registered processed egg station if they are designated Grade C or Grade Nest Run or are ungraded.
- be clearly labeled as the product of a country other than Canada.

(CFIA)

PROCESSED EGG PRODUCTS

Eggs Graded Canada C, Canada Nest run or ungraded eggs which are intended for further processing, must be transported to a processed egg station which is registered with and inspected by CFIA.

These eggs are then processed into liquid, frozen or dried form and are sold for use in the manufacture of products such as baked goods, pastas, mayonnaise, pet foods, pharmaceuticals or adhesives.

Common processed egg product definitions

Dried egg - whole egg, egg yolk or albumen in dried form.

Dried egg mix - whole egg mix or dried yolk mix.

Dried whole egg mix - dried whole egg that contains salt or a sweetening agent or both in an amount not exceeding 32% of the mix by weight.

Dried yolk mix - dried yolk that contains salt or a sweetening agent or both in an amount not exceeding 22% of the product mix by weight.

Edible - fit for human consumption.

Egg - an egg of a domestic chicken or domestic turkey.

Egg product - a dried, frozen or liquid food that contains at least 50% by weight of frozen egg, frozen egg mix, liquid egg, liquid egg mix, dried egg, or dried egg mix.
(CFIA, Canadian Egg Marketing Agency)

Egg solid - egg yolk or albumen that contains, or egg yolk and albumen that contain, no shell or water.

Size Designation	Egg Weighs Not Less Than	Egg Weighs Less Than
Jumbo	70 grams	---
Extra Large	64 grams	---
Large	56 grams	---
Medium	49 grams	---
Small	42 grams	---
Peewee	---	42 grams

(CFIA, Canadian Egg Marketing Agency)

Frozen egg - whole egg, egg yolk or albumen in a frozen form.

Frozen egg mix - liquid egg mix in a frozen form.

Inedible egg - an egg that is not suitable for human consumption.

Inedible processed egg - processed egg that is not suitable for consumption.

Liquid egg - whole egg, egg yolk or albumen in liquid form.

Liquid egg mix - liquid egg that contains salt or a sweetening agent or both in an amount not exceeding 12% of the mix by weight.

Prepackaged product - processed egg that is packed in a container in a manner that it may be sold without being re-packaged.

Process - breaking eggs, filtering, blending, heat treating, stabilizing, mixing, cooling, freezing or drying processed eggs.

Processed egg - frozen egg, frozen egg mix, liquid egg, liquid egg mix, dried egg, dried egg mix or egg product.

Processed egg station - a place in which eggs are processed.

Stabilize - to remove sugar from liquid egg.

Whole egg - the albumen and yolk of an egg but not the shell.

Whole egg mix - frozen or liquid whole egg that contains salt or a sweetening agent or both in an amount not exceeding 12% of the mix by weight.

Yolk mix - frozen or liquid yolk that contains salt or a sweetening agent or both in an amount not exceeding 12% of the mix by weight.
(CFIA)

Canadian Egg Production and Marketing System

As with chicken and turkey, eggs are produced and marketed in Canada under a system known as supply management. Under this federal-provincial agreement, each provincial egg marketing agency is assigned an annual quota of eggs to produce. The Canadian Egg Marketing Agency, in consultation with egg processors and retail and food service sector representatives, determines the annual quota. Each provincial agency then assigns quotas to the producers within its province. *(Canadian Egg Marketing Agency)*

Study Guide

Summary

What is "Inspection" and are all poultry and eggs inspected in Canada?

- Inspection is the process of ensuring that food products are free of disease or contamination and are fit for human consumption.
- In Canada, poultry and eggs that will cross provincial boundaries or be exported must be inspected for wholesomeness by the Canadian Food Inspection Agency (CFIA).
- Poultry and eggs that will not trade outside the province in which they were produced may or may not be inspected for wholesomeness, depending on provincial regulation. Some provinces have their own inspection agencies, some contract CFIA to perform food inspection services and some provinces do not require food to be inspected before retail sale.
- Poultry and eggs that have been inspected by CFIA will have this indicated by a distinctive legend on the box, case or

carton, or on the wrapping in the case of individually wrapped poultry.

What is "Grading" and are all poultry and egg products graded in Canada?

- Grading is an indicator of the quality of poultry and eggs.
- "Canada A" and "Canada Utility" are the most common grades of poultry in food service use.
- Grading of poultry is not mandatory and commonly used poultry products such as skinless, boneless chicken breasts, or chicken wings are often processed from ungraded birds.
- Poultry products which have been graded will have this clearly indicated by a distinctive logo on the box or case, or on the wrapping in the case of individually wrapped poultry.
- Eggs for retail sale must be graded and will have this clearly indicated by a distinctive logo on the box, case or carton. Canada A and Canada B are the only grades of eggs available for retail sale.
- Only Canada A eggs are sized and the size will be clearly indicated on the box or case.

Terms for Review

Federal inspection	Poultry grades
Egg grades	CFIA
HACCP	Inspection legend
Grading logos	Egg grading station
Supply management	Egg sizes
National meat inspection standard	
Provincial inspection	

Questions for Discussion

1. Are all meat, egg and poultry products produced in Canada inspected for whole someness before retail sale?
2. What are the implications of this for the food service industry?
3. Do you feel that Canada's systems of meat, poultry and egg inspection are adequate to ensure a safe and high quality food supply?
4. Should this country adopt a National Domestic Standard for meat and poultry slaughter, processing and inspection? If so, is there anything which would hinder the implementation of such a standard?
5. Is it always necessary or desirable to purchase inspected poultry for use in your kitchen?
6. Is it always necessary or desirable to purchase graded poultry for use in your kitchen?

Resources & Further Information

Alberta Ostrich Breeders Association,
73 Mohawk Road,
Lethbridge, Alta.,
T1K 5J5
www.ostrichcentre.com

B. C. Ministry of Agriculture and Food,
P.O. Box 9120,
Victoria, B.C.,
V8W 9E4
www.agf.gov.bc.ca

B. C. Turkey Marketing Board,
No.106-19329 Enterprise Way,
Surrey, B.C.,
V3S 6J8
www.columbia-valve.bc.ca/home/bcfa/ind-turkey.htm

Canadian Egg Marketing Agency,
Suite 1900, Queen Street,
Ottawa, Ont.,
K1R 5A3
www.canadaegg.ca

Canadian Food Inspection Agency,
59 Camelot Drive,
Nepean, Ont., K1A 0Y9
www.cfia.agr.ca

**Canadian Food Inspection System
Initiative,** 174 Stone Road West,
Guelph, Ont,
N1G 4S9
www.cfis.agr.ca

Canadian Turkey Marketing Agency,
969 Derry Road East,
Mississaugua, Ont.,
L5T 2J7
www.canturkey.ca

Chicken Farmers of Canada,
300 - 377 Dalhousie Str.,
Ottawa, Ont.,
K1N 9N8
www.cdn-chicken.com

Hills Foods Ltd., Burnaby, B.C.,
No. 109 - 3650 Bonneville Place,
Burnaby, B.C.,
V3N 4T7
www.hillsfoods.com

Manitoba Chicken Producer Agency,
430-A Dovercourt Dr.,
Winnipeg, Man.,
R3Y 1N4
www.chicken.mb.ca

Manitoba Turkey Producers,
430-A Dovercourt Dr.,
Winnipeg, Man.,
R3Y 1N4
www.turkey.mb.ca

Northern Goose Processors Ltd.,
P.O. Box 510,
Teulon, Man.,
R0C 3B0

Acknowledgements

*Without the help and assistance of the following
persons and organizations this chapter would
not have been possible:*

The Canadian Food Inspection Agency

**The Canadian Food Inspection System
Implementation Group**

B.C. Turkey Marketing Board

Canadian Egg Marketing Agency

Canadian Ostrich Association

Canadian Turkey Marketing Agency

Chicken Farmers of Canada

**Mr. Mark Hills, Proprietor - Hills Foods
Ltd., Burnaby, B.C.**

Manitoba Chicken Marketing Agency

Manitoba Turkey Producers

Northern Goose Producers

4

Canadian Fish and Seafood

by Roy W. Blundel

What's In It For Us

• As a young aspiring Canadian Chef, do you want information about one of Canada's greatest resources—freshwater and the fish that live in our lakes and rivers?
• Do you want to understand ways of preserving and maximizing these resources?
• Do you want to know how to choose Canadian fish and shellfish in your future endeavours?

This module will provide you with an overview of fish and seafood available in Canada.

Learning Guide

Goal: This module will give you an introduction to the resources found across our country, giving an insight into the possibilities for the Canadian Foodservice industry using our own natural resources.

Learning Outcome: After completing this module, you will be able to identify some of the possibilities working with Canadian products.

Learning Objectives: As you progress through this module you will learn about:

Types of Canadian Sea fish:	East Coast	West coast
Types of Canadian Freshwater fish:	Lake	River
Types of Canadian shellfish:	East Coast	West Coast
Preserving methods of fish and seafood:	Salted	Smoked	Canned

General formats of purchasing and preservation for the Canadian market

Resources concerning Canadian Fish and seafood:
    Associations
    Provincial Government
    Federal Government
Current and future trends in the Canadian food-service industry:
    Environment
    Chefs Creating Trends

Prerequisite: You should have a theoretical and practical understanding of basic fish and seafood preparations. You should be able to: 1. Explain how the cooking qualities of fish are affected by its lack of connective tissue. 2. Identify the freshness in a fish. 3. Recognize the basic market forms of fish and seafood. 4. Select appropriate cooking methods for fat and lean fish.

There are many species found in Canadian waters, but we have concentrated on main species used in the Canadian foodservice sector and their methods of preservation. This does not take away the importance of other product knowledge. By necessity we are constantly discovering or rediscovering the importance of lesser known species.

Main Types of Canadian Sea Fish

East Coast

Cod	Cusk	Eels
Flounder	Haddock	Hake
Halibut	Sea herring	Mackerel
Pollock	Ocean perch	Smelt
Salmon*(Atlantic)*	Sardines	Tuna
Turbot		

West Coast

Cod*(Grey)*	Cod*(Black Sablefish)*	Flounder
Halibut	Sea herring	Ling Cod
Salmon*(Pacific)*	Smelt	Sole
Tuna		

Main Types of Canadian Freshwater Fish

Arctic Char	Bass*(White)*	Bullhead
Burbot	Eels	Goldeye
Lake Herring	Lake Trout	Mullet
Perch*(Yellow)*	Pickerel*(Walleye pike)*	Pike
Sauger	Smelt	Sturgeon
Tomcod	Tullibee*(Cisco)*	Whitefish

SALMON

Of all the possible varieties of fish available, salmon, sole and a few others are recognized around the world by gourmets and chefs as being exceptional for their flavour and versatility when it comes to choice as a food item. Of all the Canadian fish available, salmon is the most popular. It is imperative to become familiar with it as, at one time or another, one will handle some kind of salmon.

Salmon is a migratory fish of which there are several species found in both the Atlantic and the Pacific areas. Atlantic salmon, as can be seen by its name, is actually the true salmon (trout belong also to this family); however, the five species found in the Pacific are still referred to as salmon.

Most salmon are anadromous, that is they live in the sea yet travel inland up rivers to spawn in fresh water. They have a built-in sense that allows them to return to their birth place as part of a cycle. Generation after generation returns to the same spot. Atlantic salmon continue this cycle many times, yet Pacific salmon unfortunately only complete the cycle once and after depositing and fertilizing their eggs, they die. Certain Atlantic salmon, although they follow a similar cycle regularly, do not return to the sea. They are known as *Landlocked* salmon. There are several types found in Canadian lakes. These are regarded as somewhat inferior since their diet is limited and they are consequently smaller in size. There are also several landlocked varieties of Pacific salmon, Coho being probably the one most well known. Regular salmon eat very little whilst in fresh water, subsequently they are at their prime just prior to the spawning season.

The time of year when caught, the location, and consequently the food and algae eaten, and how they are fished, all have direct bearing on the quality of the salmon in question. Flesh colour and texture, oil content, water content, flavour, etc., are all important issues, especially when it comes to various commercial preparations such as canning, freezing, smoking, etc.

There are several different types that vary in size and quality and each has its own characteristics. Some are better for smoking than others whilst some are preferable for canning. The salmon family is quite a complex area to cover quickly. However, as a guide to chefs, here is a simplified breakdown of the various types and their uses.

SPECIES OF SALMON
(including alternate Canadian names by which they are known)

SPECIES	NAMES	CANADIAN

ATLANTIC SALMON **N.B.** belong to same family as trout	Atlantic Salmon/Saumon de l'Atlantique (*Salmo Salar*)	a) Gaspé Bay Salmon (S.E. Quebec, near Gulf of St.Lawrence)
		b) Restigouche Salmon (River-Northern New Brunswick near Gulf of St.Lawrence
		c) Landlocked Varieties (poorer quality flesh)
		   i) Sebago Salmon (Salar -Sebago) Found between New Hampshire, USA and New Brunswick
		   ii)Quaniche Salmon (Salar Quaniche) Found in Lake St. John, Canada

PACIFIC SALMON	1. Spring Salmon/ Saumon quinnat (*Oncorhynchus tshaytscha*)	a) Chinook Salmon b) King Salmon c) Black Salmon d) Chub Salmon e) Tyee (for those weighing over 13 kg)
	2. Chum Salmon/Saumon keta (*Oncorhynchus keta*)	a) keta Salmon b) Dog Salmon c) Qualla d) Calico Salmon e) Fall Salmon
	3. Pink Salmon/Saumon Rose (*Oncorohynchus orbuscha*)	**N.B.** known in the U.S. as Humpback Salmon
	4. Sockeye Salmon/ Saumon Rouge (*Oncorohynchus nerka*)	Commonly referred to simply as Pacific Salmon
	5. Coho Salmon/ Saumon coho (*Oncorohynchus kisutch*)	a) Blue back b) Silverside c) Jack salmon d) Medium Red Salmon

Trout

A member of the salmon family, its quality is as diverse as the number of species. Flesh colour varies from white to deep red depending on molluscs and crustaceans eaten.

Arctic Char

While not a true trout, it is a relative of the brook trout. Flesh colour varies from white to red depending on diet and season, but the best are the darker fleshed. Extremely rich and fine textured, its usually bright orange to red flesh can be prepared with all cooking mediums.

Brook Trout

When of good quality, generally considered the finest trout at the table. The flesh can be white (farmed) to deep orange red (wild).

Brown Trout

This is of variable quality. The flesh colour is usually white to pale orange. The anadromus sea-run Brown is generally of much better quality, at times rivalling the best salmons.

Golden Trout

This very beautiful fish has a pale orange to red flesh and is fatter than most trout. Its fat content is not as high as lake trout.

Lake Trout

While the average weight is 10-20 lb it can be caught up to 100 lb. Flesh varies from white to red and is much fattier than other trout, although fat content is variable (the larger the fish the fattier it is).

Farmed Rainbow Trout

The most widely cultured, it was originally natural to western Canada. Flesh is mostly white when farmed although some wild stocks run from pale orange to deep red.

Main Types of Shellfish

MOLLUSCS

ABOLONE (haliofidae)

The univalve abolone is not a filter feeder (as are bivalves): It is, therefore, " immune" to red tide (gonyaulax) and does not build up bacterial concentrations in polluted waters. It is used sliced into steaks and pounded to soften and release fragrant whole "milk".

A major market area is the American West Coast. Quantities are landed in British Colombia and Alaska.

Product Forms

Frozen: cleaned whole; beaten out and cut into steaks, R.T.C., breaded steaks.
Fresh: whole, cleaned whole.

CLAMS

There are three categories in which clams may be classified:

1. Hard-shells (Atlantic and Pacific)
2. Softshells
3. Sea or surf clams

Clams are filter feeders (as are oysters, mussels, scallops)—they pump in food and water, filter the food, and pump out the water. They, therefore, can be carriers of red tide, bacteria (from pollution), etc.

If clams (hard-shell) don't close when touched or if siphon clams (the ones with "necks") don't constrict when touched, *discard* them as they are dead and no longer safe for consumption.

Hard-shell: can be eaten raw on the half-shell or in chowders.

Soft-shell: more often are steamed or fried. Clam liquor is sold as clam juice, diluted as clam broth or; concentrated (by evaporation) as clam nectar.

Atlantic Hard-shells

Atlantic hard-shells are marketed by size. Counts are commonly served as:

Name	Counts per 60 lb bushel[1]	Use
Little necks	450 - 600	raw on the half
Cherrystones	300 - 400	steamed or baked, clams casino
Topnecks	200	
Quahogs or Chowder clams	125	chopped or diced for chowder
Pumpkins	greater than 120	

[1] *There is no consistency to these size grades or counts. Every geographic region has its own definition of each of these sizes.*

Pacific Hard-shells

Manila Clams (*topes or Venerupis japonica*): commonly marketed as littlenecks or Japanese littlenecks and black clams. The Pacific is distinct from Atlantic littleneck.

They are most tender on the west coast, but not noted for half-shell. Steamed, butter dipped.

Rock Clams (*protothaca staminea*): A close relative to the manila clam, rock clams may also be sold as littlenecks, native littleneck and butter clams. They are small and tender or large and tough. Fry, steam, chowder (large) and smoked.

Soft-shell Clams (*Mya arenaria*)

Harvested from tidal flats along the Atlantic coast from North Carolina to Labrador, they go by numerous names depending on the region and use: steamers, Ipwich, Manninose, mud clams, or belly clams.

Softshells have a thin brittle shell. They are elongated in shape and are unable to close their shells tightly against a siphon. Commonly served steamed or fried or raw with lemon juice or cocktail sauce if small enough.

Market Classification:

Count per bushel	Meats per gallon
Large	400
Steamers	400 - 600
Large, shucked	200 - 250
Medium, shucked	350 - 400

Razor clams are limited in quantity and are not offered in frozen form. Razor backs have an elongated soft-shell and are chewy. East: steamed; West: fried.

Product forms:

Live: sold by the bushel, shucked per gallon. Live softshells are generally too expensive to be used for chowders.

Frozen: I.Q.F. breaded meats R.T.C. (24/ 4 oz (113g), 18/6 oz. (170g)); whole fryers or Ipwich clams.

Sea Clams

These are the most important clam fishery product yielding the largest volume of landings.

• Surf clams *(spisula solidissima)*: beach clams, skimmers, giant clams, sea clams and bar are used in chowders, cut into strips, breaded and fried or minced for canning. Their white abductor has the texture and flavour of scallops.

• Ocean quahogs *(Arctic islanica)*: mahogany quahogs, mahogany clams, black quahogs. The meat from this species is much darker than spisula.

• Pacific Northwest Goeduck - pronounced Gooey-duck *(Panope generose)*: The largest clam at 8 inches/230cm or 5 lb./2.2Kg, it is so large a siphon cannot withdraw into shell (extension up to 3 feet/90cm it is sliced, pounded, and fried as cutlets).

Product Forms:

Live: sold by bushel, chopped or minced meat.

Frozen: chopped or minced clam meat; most chopped or minced clam meats are put through a 3/8" grinder. The whole animal is minced unless stomachs are full of algae. Mantles have been used separately for clam strips.

Meat percentage in chopped clams varies:
50/50   50% meat; 50% juice
70/30   70% meat; 30% juice
dry pack   90% meat; 10% juice
Clam strips (breaded), raw unbreaded strips of clam's mantle (1/4" x 3/8" x 4" long) 6.4mm x 9.5mm x 101mm. It is possible to make clam strips from squid.

Storage:

Live clams should be stored at approximately 40°F/ 4.5°C (7 to 10 days) They should not be stored in a dry or airtight room as they need oxygen and moisture to survive. Also never put clams in fresh water as they will soon die. Shucked clams should have plump meats and clear liquid.

MUSSELS

These Bivalves can be found in both fresh and saltwater, but only saltwater mussels are suitable for eating. The most common species is the blue mussel. They are tangy, almost smoky and nutritious (12% protein, 2% fat, 4 to 8% carbohydrate). They are also rich in vitamins, especially A and minerals such as iron, copper, calcium, phosphorous. Mussels are best before spawning (in fall), winter and early spring. Generally, breeded (cultivated) mussels are smaller, but more tender and delicately flavoured than wild mussels. Prepare as one would clams or oysters. Live mussels remain tightly closed (discard open mussels). However, they will "gape" to temperature changes (e.g. refrigerature to room temperature). To test, gently try to "slide" shells across one another. If they move, discard. Discard any mussels that do not open upon cooking.

BLUE MUSSELS *(Mytilus edulis)*

Virtually all mussels on the commercial market in Canada are blue mussels. They come from both Pacific Northwest coast and the Maritimes.

Product Forms:
• Washed live: by the bushel
• Shucked frozen: I.Q.F. meats R.T.E., breaded R.T.C. meats.
• Canned: smoked

Storage:
Live they should be kept at 32°F/0°C (7 days) in a manner that will let them breathe and drain (onion bags or burlap). Under refrigeration, they should be covered lightly with ice or damp towelling. The byssus (Beard) should not be removed as it weakens the animal.

OYSTERS

Proximity to fresh water determines their flavour to large extent. Oysters feed on one-celled plants known as diatoms (these are nourished by minerals in the water and in turn nourish oyster, determining its colour, texture and flavour).

Idealists eat only half shell, brightening with lemon juice and frown upon the common use of cocktail sauce. Do not eat spawning oysters—they are edible, but inferior; excessive production of glycogen in spawning turns the meat milky, mushy and dull tasting. The best months for harvesting oysters in general are those with an "r" in them (especially in fall and winter). Half-shell oysters should be held on crushed ice as cold as possible.

Four types of oysters on a significant commercial basis:

Types of oysters	Remarks	Market sizes/Name	Meat counts per gallon
1. Eastern *(Crassostrea virginica)*	Variously called blue point, Cape Cod, Malpeque, Long Island, etc., depending on where they are harvested. Indian River considered very delicate.	1. Extra large or counts 2. Large or extra select 3. Medium or selects 4. Standard or small 5. Very small	160 161 - 200 201 - 300 (frying) 301 - 400 over 500
2. Pacific *(Crassostrea gigas)*	Similar in appearance and taste to virginica. Larger, but milder in taste. *Grading may vary from supplier to supplier.*	1. Large 2. Medium 3. Small 4. Extra small	under 65 65 - 96 97 - 144 over 144
3. Olympia *(Ostrea lurida)*	These are rare and expensive. They are miniature in size (2 in. in length) and they are considered a delicacy.		
4. Belon *(Ostrea endlis)*	Newly introduced European oyster to both coasts for aquaculture.		

Product forms:
- Live shucked: meats per gallon, whole per bushel.
- Frozen: I.Q.F. breaded meats, I.Q.F. meats, frozen of half shell. Oysters freeze very well.
- Canned: smoked

Storage:
- Live: 35^{0}F to 40^{0}F (7 to 10 days) with the cupped shell down.
- Shucked: 35^{0}F to 40^{0}F (7 days)
- Frozen: 10 to 12 months

SCALLOPS

There is a distinction between the American scallop and the French Coquille St-Jacques.

The American scallop is somewhat sweet and suggestive of a nutlike fragrance, but only the abductor muscle is used; scallops have but one abductor and cannot close tightly. They dry out rapidly once removed from water; it is therefore economically unfeasible to use the entire animal for human consumption (used for feeds and fertilizers).

The French Coquille, however, is not only entirely eaten (prep methods as for other Bivalves) but is much sweeter and more delicate. Its coral tongue, absent from the American species, is a highly prized delicacy. There are approximately 400 species, but only 12 are used commercially. There are generally 3 basic groups—cape (smallest, most delicate), bay and sea (the largest, most abundant, and therefore the most commercially important - e.g., Aleutian weathervane).

Methods of cooking:
The previous cautions on cooking seafood apply particularly to the scallop. It should be served immediately upon cooking. Usual methods include pan-frying, deep-frying (breaded or tempura), poaching, broiling and for making soups and stews. Scallops are marketed in three general categories *(see chart below).*

Product forms:
- Live whole: per bushel or count per container.
- Shucked: standard grading of scallops:
  - counts per pound (sold in gallon containers)
  - under 10 (very rare)
  - 10/20 or 10/25
  - 15/25
  - 20/30
  - 30/40 or 30/50
  - 50/70
  - 70/90
  - pieces
  most packers allow 10-15% pieces with regular scallops.

Storage:
- Fresh: may be held on ice for several days (35^{0}F to 40^{0}F).
- Frozen: held at minus 20^{0}F, should maintain quality for 1 year.

Types of scallops	Remarks	Grading	Size
1. Sea and 2. Bay	Distinguished biologically as different species, however, market designation is related to size.	Sea Bay Calicos	20 - 40 Ct. / lb. 70 - 90 Ct. / lb. average 120 Ct. / lb.
3. Calico	The Canadian sea supply harvested off Georgian Bank, and Pacific B.C.		20 - 40 Ct. / lb. 40 - 90 Ct. / lb.

RAYS

Although rays are not molluscs, they are included here for a purpose. Usually the smaller ones are used (i.e., the giant manta ray excluded). They are related closely to the shark (see lean fish). The point to be made is that most rays feed on molluscs, a fact reflected in their creamy flesh.

The edible portion of rays and skates are the "wings" which contain a firm, creamy meat so similar to scallops in texture and flavour it has been marketed for years as a scallop substitute. The wings are "punched" with an instrument similar to a cookie cutter and perfectly round cylinders similar to a large (sea) scallop are produced. Ray may be pan-fried or sautéed as cutlets, but poaching is the most common method used. Other scallop substitutes may be shark, tilefish, and flounder.

SQUID

A highly specialized mollusc with 10 arms and a long cigar-shaped body. Some actually can "fly" over the surface of the water! Squid is a voracious predator, but this lends quality to its flesh. 80% of it is edible (a very high percent) with about 18% protein. It is highly nutritious and tremendously abundant, yet it is under-utilized with an annual potential catch estimated at 100 to 300 million tons.

Marketed fresh, frozen, salted, semi-preserved, sun-dried (rubbery), and canned, squid has a delicate firm flesh that yellows slightly upon cooking. It can be pan-fried, deep-fried, stirfried, baked or boiled. Classically, small squid is cooked whole (frequently stuffed) and large is cut into rings and chunks (body only is used). Squid is also cooked in its own ink (Spain) and it is used in paella.

The edible parts of the squid are the tentacles, the mantle (body), and the wings. The skin covering the wings that contains glands which allow the animal to change colour is usually removed. Many packers "bleach" squid by soaking it in iced water before freezing.

Types and origins of squids	Characteristics
1. North Atlantic Loligo (*Loligo peallei*) flesh	• long finned squid with a light coloured • layer packed in 10 kg or 20 kg boxes
2. North Atlantic Illex (*Illex illecebrosus*)	• illex variety sells for approximately 1/5 of the price of loligo • short-finned squid generally large and darker and tougher • main landings in Canada
3. Pacific Coast	• 7 inches in length; bleached and packed whole (frozen)

Crustaceans

SHRIMP

This is the most valuable seafood product with hundreds of species, both fresh and saltwater.

They are basically from two areas from the Gulf and from the Canadian Pacific.

Several basic species are of commercial importance (Gulf and Atlantic):

1. brown
2. pink: which may also be light brown, resembling the brown
3. white
4. Caribbean white: more greyish white variously tinged with green, red and blue
5. Sea bob: especially around Hatteras; red or pinkish red alive but will turn black when cooked or frozen
6. Royal red: usually deep red but may be pinkish grey
7. Rock shrimp: brownish on top, pale on sides

The Pacific coast yields 2 pinks and 3 varieties of prawns (very large shrimp, side-stripe and spot shrimp).

The common "green" shrimp is not really a species, but a term used for most "fresh" shrimp (or fresh-frozen with heads removed) including pinks and whites.

Shrimp that are fresh are firm and of a rather sweet, "fresh" smell. A stale shrimp will smell of ammonia (as will lobster and crayfish). If one shrimp smells, the chances are the rest in the package are also stale. Some shrimp may taste of iodine (e.g., brown shrimp from which some of the brown colour also comes). This may be natural (of sea shrimp; brackish water contains less amounts of iodine while fresh water shrimp are consistently sweet and iodine-free) or may be due to the use of the preservative sodium bisulphate (illegal in Canada but used in other countries). Generally, shrimp have more iodine than other crustaceans, but also are high in vitamins and minerals. They are 20.5% protein.

COLOURS AND TYPES OF SHRIMP (Native to Canadian waters)

Types of Shrimp	Origin or other names	Colour	Size
Northern (*pandalus borealis*)	Northern Shrimp Salad shrimp Matane shrimp	pink	• 26/30, 35/45, 45/55 • usual counts are per pound or "sea run" meaning ungraded

CANADIAN LOBSTER

This crustacean has 10 legs, including two large front claws. The body and tail are hard-shelled and the spiky antenna are as long as the body. The front claws are filled with meat, and one part of the claw is very large, flat and heavy while the other is smaller and thinner. All lobster meat is firm, but the tail meat is firmer than meat from the claws. It has a sweet, mild flavour. Lobsters are native to all East Coast Provinces and the main season is from the end of April to mid-July.

Live Lobsters are classified by size:

Canners	170-454	grams	1/2-1lb
Chicks(chix)	450-500	grams	1- 1 1/8 lb.
Eights	500-570	grams	1-1 1/8-1 1/4 lb.
Quarteers	570-680	grams	1 1/4-1 1/2 lb.
Halves	680-800	grams	1 1/2 -1 3/4 lb.
Select	800-900	grams	1 3/4- 2 lb.
Deuces	900-1135	grams	2 -2 1/2 lb.
Small Jumbos	1135-1475	grams	2 1/2-3 1/4 lb.
Medium Jumbos	1475-2270	grams	3 1/4-5 lb.
Large Jumbos	2270-&-over		5 lb.-&-over

SNOW CRAB

Among several species if crab, snow crab (opilo) has thin legs, red dorsal shells and tan to brown ventral (bottom) shells. Snow crab have four pairs of legs and a pair of claws.

Preserved Fish and Seafood

SALTED

Heavy Salted

Fish are headed and gutted and their backbone bones are removed. The split fish are piled in layers with a mixture of coarse and fine salt between each layer, using about 30lb (13.5kg) salt to every 100lb (45kg) of fish. The fish are then hung in a current of air, or machine dried.

Light-cured

Fish are headed, gutted, washed and split, and about one-third of the fish is salted with dry salt, using 8 to 10lb (3.5kg to 4.5kg) salt to every 100lb (45kg) fish. The fish are laid in tubs until the juices dissolve the salt and form brine, in which the fish remain from two to three days. They are then sun or machine dried.

SMOKED FISH

Commercially speaking fish smoking is mainly limited to certain types, such as salmon, trout, codfish, herring, whitefish, eel, sturgeon.

Nevertheless, there are still many more varieties that are smoked but are often found only in small amounts as regional specialities. Prime examples would be Winnipeg Goldeye (Smoked Ciscoe), or smoked shark.

Distribution of smoked fish world-wide requires extensive product knowledge and experience in its preparations as well as the need for expensive equipment and plants, to ensure product consistency, which is of prime importance. Yet, the scope of the subject still allows the Chef to experiment with smoking, using often only an old converted refrigerator as a smokehouse.

Originally, smoking and drying were done simply to increase the life expectancy of food. However, today through improved processes along with our refined palettes, its popularity is owed more to the enhanced flavour and the fact we have an optional way of eating the product.

Today there are, in general, two methods of smoking food products— both use fairly large amounts of salt and both are excellent to use for fish. They are Hot Smoking and Cold Smoking.

The ultimate product, as you will understand shortly, is extremely dependant on the method used. Other factors which influence this immensely are how the salt is applied; which type of fuel is used; the temperature variance; and, of course, the time span of the processes. To understand this more closely, let's break down the subject in sections and examine each in more detail.

Hot Smoking

In this process, the temperature ranges from as low as 120° F(48.9°C) to 180⁰F(82.2°C). This increases gradually, usually at intervals of half an hour or so. The time needed can vary from as little as 6 hours to as much as 12 hours. Factors that govern this include the size of the fish, the closeness to the fire and, of course, the desired effect and cure. This method actually "cooks" the fish; that is to say that all the protein present in it becomes totally coagulated (this takes place when the internal temperature exceeds 140°F/60°C). When prepared in this way the finished product has a short lifespan unless refrigerated.

In a way, this process can be compared to barbecuing, although there are obvious differences. In barbecuing, the product is not salted as much. The product is kept nearer the fire or heat source and consequently, because of this higher temperature (200°F/93.3°C), the process takes less time. Nevertheless, both methods result in a final product that is "cooked".

Prior to smoking in this way, the fish must be salted in one way or another. This can be achieved by covering with dry salt or by soaking in liquid brine. These two methods of salt application will be explained in more detail shortly.

Cold Smoking

This is a much more specialized process in which the product is not actually cooked. By using a temperature of 70-90⁰F (21C-32.2⁰C) for a longer period of time, the product is dried out and cured with minimal protein coagulation, yet it still retains a mild smoke flavour. This process also requires the addition of salt to help preservation, enhance flavour and increase life expectancy. This again can be achieved by dry salting or the use of a brine.

The Application of Salt Prior to Smoking

The application of salt is an integral part of the smoking process and, as previously mentioned, there are two ways of doing this: using dry salt, or liquid brine. Before examing these more closely, let us understand what salt does. Salt (Sodium Chloride) through osmosis (the diffusion of a fluid through a semi-permeable membrane resulting in equalization of the pressure on each side), removes body fluids from the fish, replacing them with salt. Eliminating this moisture deprives spoilage bacteria of their natural environment. At the same time, however, salt will penetrate the fish and, along with the smoke, will enhance the flavour of the fish, giving it the notable characteristics which have made smoked products so famous. Smoke increases the tensile strength of connective tissue, yet if too hot, along with excessive moisture, it will do the reverse and either weaken it, or destroy it before the curing action has had time to take place.

Dry Salting

The most important point to mention here is that only pure salt be used. Table salt, for example, contains additives which keep it "free running" and moisture free. These cause the fish protein to coagulate and in most cases, particularly "smoked salmon", this is to be avoided. Kosher salt is one of the best available. The fish should be covered with salt and left to sweat. Time varies with fish size and cure desired. Following this process, the salt is rinsed off, the fish dried and then smoked as required.

Salmon

Salmon can be smoked in this way (6-8 hours), although "smoked salmon" as we know it today usually consists of filets that are dry salted and cold smoked over a considerably longer period of time.

This method is highly recommended in the preparation of smoked salmon sides or similar filets of other large fish. First, the filets are washed to remove all the blood. Then the skin side (remember salmon skin is usually scored) is sprinkled with salt enough to adhere. The filet is then inverted and the flesh side is covered with salt 1/16"-1/8" deep over the thick part of the filet with considerably less on the tail end. If the filets are to be hung whilst smoking, it is not even necessary to salt the tail since salt, along with moisture, will run down the filet, salting the tail sufficiently.

Salmon filets are usually left covered with this salt for 8-24 hours as required. They are then rinsed off, hung and air dried, and smoked. In some cases just prior to smoking they are marinated with sugar and rum and/or special herbs to further enhance the flavour of the finished product.

Brine Method

This method of salting is not widely practised for smoked salmon. However, it is excellent for many other types of fish. It is simply the practice of soaking the fish to be smoked in a brine (salt) solution prior to smoking. Again, once this process is complete, the fish is rinsed in cold water and hung to air dry before smoking.

The strength of the brine is around 70°-80° solution. A Salinometer (a type of hydrometer) is used to measure the percentage of salt in the brine.

A 70° solution consists of two cups of salt to 1 gallon of water and usually one cup of sugar added to it. Other optional additives may be used, such as garlic (1tsp per gallon), liquid onion (1tsp per gallon), lemon or lime juice (1/4 cup per gallon), Tabasco (1tsp per gallon), and pickling spice (1oz. per gallon previously boiled in a little water and left to cool).

Fish Preparation in General Prior to Smoking

Preferably use fresh fish. In certain circumstances, frozen fish that has been thawed can be used. However, as a rule, this is avoided since one can never be sure that the fish was handled properly prior to freezing. The fact that defrosting encourages the loss of moisture in itself seems fine, yet there is also flavour loss and the flesh weakens, which is of primary importance here.

Small fish can be jibbed and hung by the tail to ensure they drain during the smoking process. It is preferable, though, to open them from the belly and hang by the head. The use of "S" hooks are standard.

Large fish can be filleted or cut into pieces, hung or spiked accordingly prior to smoking. Others can be open filleted and hung ready for smoking. Others are smoked on racks, turning them occasionally to produce an even smoked product. The next question to arise is that of the smoke.

Smokehouses

Most in-house smoke houses can be built using small wooden barrels or even converted refrigerators. There are small portable outdoor smokers and small electric hot plate units available commercially. However, these tend to barbecue rather than smoke.

Small yet permanent cabinet-type smokehouses can be constructed relatively simply, bearing in mind they have the same needs as large commercial types, such as:

- The unit should be vented to insure proper circulation of smoke and air.
- Ventilation should be controlled in such a way that wood smoulders and does not flame.
- Sufficient racks, trays, hooks, etc. are needed. Bear in mind that these must be positioned to allow smoke and heat to contact all surfaces uniformly.
- Excessive direct heat must be avoided.
- Although for the experienced it may not be essential, a thermometer inserted in a cork hanging in the top of the unit is a good idea. Since the shape of the structure and the material with which it is built can affect the results, it is often necessary to adjust temperatures and times in order to achieve satisfactory results.
- If electrically operated, make sure it is grounded.
- Design the unit bearing in mind the distance of the food being smoked from the fire. As a rough guide, 4 feet is ample if using sawdust or 6 feet if using logs.

Types of Fuel Used in Smoking

Any nonresinous wood can be used, preferably "green" rather than dry. Again there are so many choices and combinations that to list them would be endless. Most popular are: oak, hickory, maple, beech, alder, and juniper. Other excellent choices would include fruitwoods such as apple, apricot, cherry or pear.

Wood used must be free from moss or bark as this makes a bitter tasting product. Wood can be utilized in several different ways. For "cold smoking" use sawdust or small chips which smoke and do not flame up too much. For "hot smoking", small logs are preferable. A few charcoal briquettes can make a useful addition to keep things in motion with very little attention.

Smoked Salmon Quality

Once smoked, the sides should be left out of the smokehouse for 24 hours to obtain peak flavour then refrigerated until required. To test for quality, place your hands at opposite sides and press ever so gently inwards. Small droplets of oil will appear between the musculature and medianline. If water appears, the salmon is under smoked; if nothing appears, the salmon is actually cooked and although possibly an excellent tasting product, is not "cold smoked salmon" as we know it.

Smoked salmon usually has a pleasant and appetizing orangy red colour which is fairly consistent due to the quality of the salmon with its characteristic red flesh. However, sometimes it is necessary, particularly in the case of spring salmon, to add a little red colour since sometimes the flesh is lacking in its natural state.

Other Smoked Fish Products

Smoked Oysters, Clams, Mussels

Usually, these are steamed in the shells for 10 minutes to make them easier to handle. The meat is then brined for 5 minutes (70^0) and then air dried on oiled wire mesh racks. When dry, it is hot smoked (100-140°F/37.8C-60°C), preferably using maple or applewoods as the fuel for about 2 1/2 to 3 hours. It can be frozen or kept refrigerated in oil (cottonseed, peanut, or olive).

Smoked Mackerel

Usually, these are split down the back, cleaned, and brined in a low salt solution (30-50°) for about 15-30 minutes depending on the size. Then they are lightly hot smoked (small 100° for 4 hours and large 150°- 200° for 6 hours). During the spring and winter, Atlantic mackerel are lower in oil than normal. Subsequently these, if smoked, produce a better smoked product which is less susceptible to rancidity. Shelf life is limited so the product is often plastic wrapped and frozen.

Smoked Herring

Due to their thin body shape, many small fish like this must be handled carefully. Ten minutes in a brine solution (80°) is sufficient once they are dressed. After this, rinse and air dry (1 hour). Hot smoke 4-6 hours depending on temperature used.

Smoked Trout

Prepare in the same manner as smoked herring. Large lake trout are cold smoked and prepared much in the same way as salmon.

Winnipeg Goldeye

This freshwater fish is similar to a lake herring or a whitefish found in the Red River, near Winnipeg.

Because of enormous weight loss during processing, to end up with a finished product of 3/4lb to 1 lb, one must start with a fish weighing in at a good 1 1/2lb. It is probably one of the only fish that improves with freezing prior to smoking. It is usually gutted and frozen for a month, defrosted in a brine, dyed and then hot smoked over oak chips. Although it can be eaten cold, amongst gourmets, it is preferred to be eaten hot, especially when prepared "en papillotte".

Smoked Shrimps and Prawns

Popular in North West Canada, the best way to prepare them is to shell them prior to smoking. This avoids moisture build up under the shell, which tends to toughen them. Brining takes only about 10 minutes (80°solution). They are air dried like mussels oysters etc., and are hot smoked for about 1-1 ½ hours (80°-140°F/26.7C-60°C).

CANNED

Various fish and seafood products are commercially canned. To further investigate some of their commercial forms refer to the next section.

Smoked Oysters
Smoked Mussels
Sardines
Clams
Anchovies
Pink Salmon
Sockeye Salmon
Lobster
Crab

General Formats of Purchasing and Preservation

Canadian Fisheries produce fish in great variety. The product, however, is highly perishable and transport across the country is a major industry problem. The Fisheries Research Board of Canada, the foodservice industry and those concerned with transportation are continually working on improving methods of refrigeration in transportation.

Through the development of quick freezing and the wide use of frozen storage throughout the country, the supply of fish to all of the foodservice industry is constantly increasing. Fresh fish packed in ice can be shipped by rail, refrigerated transport or by air freight to the larger metropolitan areas.

Spoilage of fish may be delayed by chemical methods which are permitted in the fishing industry in prescribed amounts regulated by the Foods and Drugs Act. Sodium Nitrate is the only food preservative permitted, but two antibiotics are also permitted: chlortetracycline and oxytetra-cycline. Preservatives are not used on fish sold for export as they are not permitted in the countries which purchase our Canadian fish.

From time to time you may notice an odour from the fish when you first open a box and remove the paper. If this is caused by the preservative, it will soon disappear when exposed to the air in your refrigerator.

The surface of fresh fish should be washed well (though there are some exceptions). Frequent and thorough handwashing is also essential when handling fish, as the covering slime may contain pathogenic bacteria, particularly in fish from inland waters which are often polluted. Such bacteria can be transferred from the hands to other foods.

The shells of oysters and clams should be washed thoroughly outside before opening, but should never be soaked in fresh water.

When a daily supply of fresh fish and shellfish is not available, the fish and shellfish should be kept in ice in a proper fish box or a perforated container set in a large container to catch the melted ice.

SPECIES	COMMERCIAL FORMS
Canadian lobster	• **Whole:** fresh live or cooked; frozen blanched; frozen, totally cooked, in brine • **Frozen canned:** claws, tails and knuckles; claws and tails, tomalley and roe mix
Atlantic blue mackerel	• Whole fillets • Fresh, frozen, cold smoked • Hot smoked, canned, salted
Atlantic oysters	• Live in the shell • Canned smoked
Atlantic salmon	• Whole, steaks, fillets, portions, patties
Atlantic snow crab	• **Frozen** whole cooked; canned; frozen meat: leg sections, claws, salad meat • Canned hot pack
Cultured sea scallops	• **Live:** whole in shell
Herring	• Whole ungutted • Pared: head and tail removed • Fillet • Butterfly fillet: boned
Mussels	• Live: whole in shell • Frozen: in sauce
Northern shark (spiny dog fish)	• Fresh: whole headed and gutted, steaks or fillets • Frozen: idem fresh
Northern shrimp	• Fresh whole: raw or cooked; peeled, cooked • Frozen block whole (raw or cooked) • Frozen block peeled (raw or cooked) • Frozen IQF • Canned in brine; smoked; prepared dishes
Smoked salmon	• Fresh • Frozen
Steelhead salmon & trout	• Whole: head on gutted • Fillet: skin on or skinless, boneless

Resources Concerning Canadian Fish and Seafood

PROVINCIAL GOVERNMENTS

British Colombia Ministry of Fisheries
780 Blanshard St, Victoria, BC
V8V 1X4

New Brunswick Fish and Aquaculture
P.O. 6000, Fredericton, New Brunswick,
E3B 5H1

Newfoundland Seafood Education
Program
P.O. Box 8700,
St. John's, Newfoundland
A1B 4J6

Nova Scotia Fish and Aquaculture
5151 George St, 7th floor,
Halifax, Nova Scotia,
B3J 1M5

Prince Edward Island Development
and Marketing
P.O. Box 910,
Charlottetown, Prince Edward Island,
C1A 7L9

Quebec Minister of Agriculture and
Fishing/Direction générale des pêches, de
la formation et de la recherche
Secteur des communications,
96 montée Sandy Beach,
Gaspé (Québec)
G0C 1R0

Information can be found using the Federal
Resource **Central and Arctic Region** for the
following provinces:

Northwest Territories central and arctic
Ontario
Saskatchewan
Yukon
Alberta
Manitoba

FEDERAL GOVERNMENT

For questions of a general nature regarding
Fisheries and Oceans, you may contact:

Fisheries & Oceans Canada
Communications Branch
200 Kent Street
13th Floor, Station 13228
Ottawa, Ontario
K1A OE6

Pacific Region

Fisheries & Oceans
555 West Hastings Street
Vancouver, British Columbia
V6B 5G3

Central and Arctic Region

Fisheries & Oceans
501 University Crescent
Winnipeg, Manitoba
R3T 2N6

Laurentian Region

Fisheries & Oceans
P.O. Box 1550
Quebec, Quebec
G1K 7Y7

Maritime Region

Fisheries & Oceans
P.O. Box 550
Halifax, Nova Scotia
B3J 2S7

Newfoundland Region

Fisheries & Oceans
P.O. Box 5667
St John's, Newfoundland
A1X 5 X1

Current and Future Trends

ENVIRONMENT

Because of improved technologies, the total world catch of fish more than tripled during the two decades after World War II, then levelled off. Although natural causes for this decline exist, such as changes in ocean currents, human causes such as pollution and overfishing have definitely contributed. Halibut, herring, cod, salmon, anchovy, sardine, and some tuna are now being overfished.

Accurate information on the size of fish populations is hard to gather because ocean fish make long migrations or dwell too deep for a proper count to be made. Management for a sustainable yield is, therefore, very difficult. Investigators are trying to relieve the overfishing of traditional food fishes by exploring methods to process and market less popular species such as squid, hake, and pollack, or the fishes currently used for livestock food.

Ocean ranching is common in many areas and may use fish that gather for spawning. These fish are corralled with stationary weirs and can be used as food and as a source to propagate young for further ranching. These methods are commonly used for salmon in northwestern Canada, where young are released in streams and return as adults to their "home" sites.

Ultimate control of fishery production is found in aquaculture. Eggs are hatched and the fry are put into pens and fed or stocked into seminatural ponds to grow on natural foods. This process, also called mericulture, has become popular because favoured food fishes grown in this way fetch high prices. Pen culture of Atlantic salmon in Eastern Canada and harvesting of Mussels in Prince Edward Island are two examples. Culture of local fishes can also provide protein in many developing countries more efficiently and cheaply than wild fish capture. By the year 2000, 20% of fishery harvest may come from aquaculture systems.

CHEFS CREATING TRENDS

Chefs today have to be able to adapt to the reality of a fast-changing world. We are no longer able to count on standing orders for fish and seafood. A great flexibility has to be shown towards the latest market trends—for example, reworking lesser known fish into the menus. Here is an example of future species of fish and seafood from Canadian waters that one will be asked to work with in the future:

Category	Common Name	Culinary use
Saltwater	Dogfish	Filleted or cut into steaks mainly pan-fried
	Monkfish	Can be used as a filler; easily assimilates flavour of more expensive products like lobster or scallop meat
	Common Periwinkle	Marinated and served in seafood salads and stews
	Whelk	Marinated and served in seafood salads and stews
	Sea Cucumber	Smoked, dried, pickled; works well with Asian style meals
	Atlantic Wolfish	Filleted, pan-fried
	Soft-shell clam	In chowders or breaded
	Sea Urchins	Consumed raw or in speciality soup

Freshwater	Common name	Culinary use
	American Shad	Ground meat for fish stuffings
	Brown bullhead	Filler fish good for terrines and patés
	Carp	Filleted, marinated, pan-fried
	Eel	Smoked or in a stew
	Channel catfish	Filleted and pan-fried
	Rockbass	Filleted and pan-fried
	Lake sturgeon	Smoked
	Common sucker	Filleted and pan-fried
	Crayfish	Speciality soup, used instead of shrimp

Working with Canadian fish and seafood automatically leads us to complement them. Various Canadian products can be used to enhance the flavour if so required. Some of the lesser known species need to be improved. Savoury butter sauces using wildberry vinegars can improve flavour; using wild rice and grains can improve texture (an example could be to bread the fish with wild oats).

Research into native and ethnic cookery will enable you to create new trends in the way you prepare your fish dishes. Chefs must be constantly aware of new products and resources around us. It is important to use these resources supplied by the Canadian industry and our Federal and Provincial governments.

Terms for Review

Salinometer	IQF
Brine	RTC
Smoking	Salmon Pacific
Mericulture	Salmon Atlantic
Anadromous	Shuck

Questions for Discussion

1. What fish products could you preserve in your province?
2. Would it be possible to build a co-operative smokehouse in your school?
3. Have you visited a local fish farm? Do they have any new species in development?
4. Based on what you have read could you develop a truly Canadian fish and seafood theme menu?
5. How many types of Canadian fish does your local fish market provide? What tells you they have been caught in Canadian waters?

5

Culinary Arts and Vegetarianism

by Dominique and
Cindy Duby

What's In It For Us

• Do you want to have a better understanding of vegetarian concepts?
• Do you want to explore topics that help to design vegetarian meals?
• Do you want to learn how to prepare balanced vegetarian meals?

This module will provide you with a basic introduction to vegetarianism and vegetarian cuisine. Note that the nutritional information presented is not in-depth and will only briefly discuss major factors or nutrients. This module will list some examples of vegetarian media, preparation techniques and food composition concepts for you to use as a basic knowledge to build on. Please note that the original recipes used to create the vegetarian dishes of this module were not written by the authors. The authors did create the amalgamated versions from existing culinary literature so that these *new* creations would reflect some of today's modern culinary trends as well as vegetarian cuisine requirements.

Learning Guide

Goal: The purpose of this module is to provide an overview of the basic principles of vegetarian cuisine.

Learning Outcome: After completing this module, you will be able to identify some of the factors and concerns pertaining to vegetarianism and to prepare various vegetarian dishes.

Learning Objectives: As you work through this module, you will learn to:

1. *Explore vegetarian factors* - such as definitions trends and perceptions as well as basic nutritional benefits and concerns
2. *Categorize vegetarian media* - through the use of a vegetarian chef palette.
3. *Examine vegetarian menu composition factors* - such as alternative preparation techniques and the combining of textures and flavours.
4. *Prepare vegetarian dishes* - including soups, first and main courses using the recipes from this module.

Prerequisite: You should have a theoretical and practical understanding of basic cooking techniques for vegetables, starches and grains. You should be able to: 1. identify and evaluate the quality of raw products [mushrooms, herbs, produces etc.], 2. apply correct cleaning and cutting techniques, 3. apply various cooking methods, 4. evaluate correct stages of doneness, 5. understand the physical changes that occur during cooking.

Vegetarian Factors

VEGETARIAN DEFINITIONS

Vegetarianism is becoming increasingly popular in North America. Some people choose to endorse a vegetarian diet because of ethical, religious, economical or environmental reasons while others do so to achieve or maintain a better health status. Three terms are commonly used to describe the different types of vegetarian diets:

- *Lacto-Ovo*—a diet that excludes all animal flesh, but still includes *lacto*—dairy products as well as *ovo*—eggs.
- *Pure Vegetarian or Vegan*—a diet that avoids all foods of animal origin including eggs, dairy products as well as gelatin and honey.
- *Pesco and Semi or Partial*—some people associate these terms to a vegetarian diet because they refer to a diet that mainly consists of vegetarian food products. Although *pesco, semi* and *partial* diets usually exclude red meat, they still include the occasional use of fish—*pesco* or poultry and therefore they cannot be called a true vegetarian diet.

HEALTH BENEFITS

A better health status is, for most North Americans, the primary benefit associated with a vegetarian diet. The types of nutrients or foods that are used to create vegetarian meals have been recognized to have numerous health benefits. Many plants contain phytochemicals that are believed to protect against various diseases including cancer. Plants provide essential nutrients such as vitamins, minerals and dietary fibre which also help to prevent the onset of certain diseases. There are many scientific reports which state that a vegetarian diet helps to reduce the risk of heart diseases, obesity and cancer. Despite that fact, heart diseases and several types of cancer are still the primary causes of death in Canada. However, we are living longer in part due to the many advancements in modern medicine, but also because of our increasing knowledge of the link between proper nutrition and better health.

VEGETARIAN PERCEPTIONS

Vegetarian cuisine is commonly thought to be health food and thus is often perceived to be boring, bland and lacking complexity. This perception is probably one of the greatest contributing factors to the limited success that vegetarian cuisine has enjoyed thus far. However, media exposure of the health benefits and nutritional value of a vegetarian diet are leading an increasing number of consumers to demand that more alternative or healthy food choices be available on restaurants' menus. The populations of many North American cities includes an increasing number of people for whom vegetarianism is a way of life. As members of the foodservice industry, we must take note and recognize that this shift can potentially affect the success of many eating establishments, whether they be casual or fine dining.

NUTRITIONAL CONCERNS

Only a few nutritional concerns really affect the design or preparation of a vegetarian meal. The nutrient that has the potential to be of concern is *protein*. The biggest myth that has been associated with a vegetarian diet is that this type of diet does not supply enough complete protein to satisfy healthy nutritional requirements. This myth is false of course. However, there are some protein factors that should be addressed when designing *vegan* meals.

Protein is a macro-nutrient made up of long chain of 20 compounds called *amino acids* which are present in animal as well as in plant protein. Eight or nine of these amino acids are considered *essential,* meaning that they cannot be produced by the body. Therefore, these essential amino acids must be present in the food that we eat and in a sufficient amount over an entire day, but not necessarily in each meal as they will be "banked" throughout the day. This is not a concern though for lacto-ovo vegetarian diets since eggs and dairy products are sources of complete proteins. Vegans on the other hand, do not eat eggs or any other source of animal proteins and some plants may be lacking or not have a high enough amount of certain amino acids to meet vegans daily requirements. This is not a problem if the vegan meal is prepared with complete plant proteins or if it has been designed with a process called *protein combining.* Tofu and whole grains such as quinoa and amaranth offer a great source of complete protein for vegans. The protein combining process, as its name implies, consists of combining one or more sources of plant protein so that a desired amount of amino acids is reached over an entire day. For example:

- *legumes* such as lentils or peas should be combined with *whole grains* such as wheat berries, wheat flour, brown rice or barley.
- *nuts* such as peanuts or cashews should be combined with *grains* or *legumes* such as wheat germ or soybeans.

In order to establish which plant protein should be combined or to evaluate the amount needed, there are many books available complete with tables that will provide levels of protein and amino acid present as well as charts outlining the minimum daily requirements. Please refer to the bibliography section of this module for a list of books available on the subject. This evaluation can also be performed through the use of specialized nutritional analysis computer software, although this software can be rather expensive.

Vegetarian Media

VEGETARIAN CHEF'S PALETTE PROCESS

Identifying and categorizing vegetarian media such as vegetables, fruits, whole grains, herbs, spices and legumes can help chefs who are not aware of vegetarian factors to create balanced meals. These media have many culinary and sensory benefits and offer a multitude of textures, flavour, colours and shapes. However, many chefs view these ingredients only as garnishes or as a complement to animal protein and not as the dish main component. Perhaps the main reason is that chefs are not trained to create nutritionally balanced, culinary complex dishes with vegetarian media only. A *vegetarian chef palette*—an on-going list of common and exotic vegetarian ingredients available—is a very good tool to consider. A typical palette can be divided into as many categories as needed from the different types of vegetables to spices and sauces. This categorizing process helps to design vegetarian dishes or meals that have a good source of protein as well as a distinct flavours, complex texture and appealing colours. Table 1. is an example of the beginning of a Chef Palette including some examples of classifications of the properties and varieties of some exotic media.

Table 1. A Sample of a Vegetarian Chef Palette

Medium Classification	Properties	Varieties - Products
Fungi or mushrooms	Provide protein, texture, rich colours, intense flavours.	Maitake, Lion's Mane, Eryngii, Stropharia, Cauliflower, Pine, Lobster, Hedgehog...
Vegetables, roots	Slow roasted or confit they provide rich, fatty mouthfeel with many ranges of deep & earthy flavours.	Burdock, Salsify, Golden beets, Sunchoke, Jicama, Vidalia onions, Fennel, Rutabaga, Daikon...
Whole Grains & Seeds	Provide protein, fibre, crunchy textures and nutty flavours.	Kamut, Quinoa, Amaranth, Spelt, Pepitas, Kasha...
Legumes	Provide protein, rich textures and colours.	Cannellini, Black Garbanzo, Adzuki, Anasazi, Trout...
Other Starches	Provides carbohydrates and satiating properties.	Wild Mushroom Pasta, Orzo, Polenta...
Herbs - Greens	Provides flavour, colour, texture and finishing touch.	Lovage, Shiso, Dandelion, Wheat grass, Kaffir...
Vegetable, fruits	Provide multitudes of colours and flavour contrasts—sweet vs. acid.	Red curry squash, Heirloom tomatoes, Orange Heirloom Turkish eggplant...
Stems	Add texture and bulkiness.	Cardoon, Cattails, Chard...
Spices	Provide complexity	Amchur, Cardamom, Vanilla..
Alternative Protein Products	Provide meat like texture and appearance although usually low in fat or fat free.	Textured Vegetable Protein, Wheat Gluten, Tempeh, Meat Analogue....

Table 1. Continued

Medium Classification	Properties	Varieties - Products
Cheeses	Add protein, moderate to large amount of fat & rich flavours.	Gorgonzola, Haloumi, Goat, Labneh...
Oils	Adds an artistic or visual affect, rich infused flavours.	Coriander, Truffle, Wasabi...
Juices & Reductions	Vivid colours, freshness, light texture yet intense flavour.	Any vegetable juice such as carrot, zucchini.... & reductions of dark vegetable stock, wine, juices...

Vegetarian Menu Composition

DEFINE CUSTOMERS NEEDS

It is important to distinguish the purpose that a meal is trying to achieve. For example, a chef may create a vegetarian dish or menu which is based solely on *nutritional* or *health values.* The intent here would be to please customers who are concerned about particular nutrients [e.g. fat, sodium or fibre content] or preparation methods [e.g. smoked or oven roasted]. Alternatively, a chef may create a dish based on *creative* or *gastronomic culinary values,* which are intended to please discerning customers who want complex or memorable vegetarian meals. Although these two approaches—nutritional vs. culinary—are not necessarily incompatible, they must be defined so that the consumer needs are met.

THE FAT FACTOR

There is one major component that vegetarian media substantially lack in comparison to animal flesh: ***fat***. Animal fat provides a flavour and mouthfeel sensation that is not naturally matched by vegetarian mediums. From a health perspective this limitation would be considered a benefit, since vegetarian media are generally low in saturated fat and are cholesterol free. Nevertheless, oven roasting or confit preparation methods, for example, can indeed provide items such as squash, root vegetables or mushrooms that have a rich texture, glossy appearance and deep roasted colours.

MENU CREATION GUIDELINES

Some guidelines should be followed to create a *nutritionally* or *gastronomically* balanced vegetarian meal. The menu should include various preparation techniques, different textures, interesting flavour combinations, and visual appeal.

• ***Preparation techniques:*** Some vegetarian media benefit from specific preparation methods, yet a meal should include a variety of them. The balance here is to choose ingredients that complement one another and that can be prepared with different cooking methods. For example, a roasted mushrooms on a toasted barley risotto, confit of organic fennel, crispy fried julienne of onions and a fennel juice reduction.

• ***Assorted textures:*** As many senses as possible should be triggered. For example a beet chip or crispy polenta will provide some resistance to the tooth and be crunchy thus will provide gustatory as well as auditory stimuli. An open puff pastry Pithivier filled with a rich mix of colourful roasted root vegetable along with a silky smooth chestnut purée, surrounded by a glossy smoked tomato sauce drizzled with a basil oil will provide many textures variations as well as gustatory, auditory and visual stimuli.

• ***Flavour combination:*** Intense or complex flavours along with flawless techniques are necessary components in the creation of a memorable culinary experience. Yet one must not be tempted to mixed too many flavours in search of complexity. When in doubt, simplicity is probably the best approach. We all have heard of the expression "everything, but the kitchen sink" and this expression also applies to vegetarian food design. A good approach would be to start first by establishing the ***theme*** and ***grading principle*** to follow. For example the theme may be Mediterranean, Pacific West Coast or maybe just one ingredient theme such as mushrooms. The grading principle may follow a pattern of light to rich textures or of delicate to strong flavours. Although a theme is not always necessary, it will help to provide a sense of cohesion or identity to the meal. This does not imply that other ingredients, spices, cooking methods or influences should not be used or included, just use common sense. Second, establish which products are available and only purchase the freshest seasonal foodstuffs at the peak of their flavours. If possible, try to obtain certified organic produce, which exhibit much

stronger flavours. Next, design the dish-menu while using the guidelines as outlined above: preparation techniques and assorted textures. Finally, choose matching flavours to enhance the complexity of the dish—menu through the use of spices, herbs, powerful sauces or reductions and colourful oils to create a complex artistic display that stimulate both taste and sight. Table 2 provides an example of a five course fall vegetarian menu with a West Coast theme. The grading system follows a pattern of delicate to strong flavours providing many gustatory stimuli: sweet carrot to light goat cheese to stronger caramelized onions and beets to intense mushroom and roasted parsnips - peppers, finished by a richly flavoured cheesecake. Preparation techniques are varied, including poaching, braising, frying, caramelizing, reducing, roasting, confit and baking. The meal provides visual stimuli through many colour contrast as well as auditory stimuli through carrot chips, toasted pepitas, crispy potatoes, toasted barley and cheesecake crust.

Table 2. A Fall Vegetarian Menu with a West Coast theme

Carrot soup with fine herbs dumplings, garam masala butter & carrot chips.

***

Pink grapefruit, warm braised chard, pepitas and goat cheese salad.

***

Crispy potatoes Napoleon with caramelized onions & beets, lemon thyme infused white wine reduction.

***

Toasted barley & wild mushroom nage with fennel confit, roasted parsnips, red peppers and maitake mushroom.

***

Baked squash Neufchatel cheesecake flavoured with a cinnamon-orange-port wine syrup.

Source: DC Duby Hospitality Services Inc. '98.

Table 3. A Garden Menu

Salad of roasted chestnut, bitter greens, grain mustard & pomegranate seeds

***

Big ravioli with grilled fennel, rosemary & a fresh tomato juice

***

Gratin of rice beans with roasted garlic, artichoke heart & spinach

***

Chausson of cèpes and portobello mushrooms with Spanish onions, marjoram & balsamic vinegar

***

Warm potpourri of winter fruits with a spice bouquet & gingerbread

Source: Dornengurg, A., Page, K., 1996. *Culinary Artistry* New York: Van Nostrand Reinhold

Vegetarian Recipes

VEGETABLE STOCK

Yield: 1 qt.-1*l*   Portions

US	METRIC	INGREDIENTS	PROCEDURE
4 oz	125 g	Onion	1. Wash and trim the vegetables. Chop coarsely.
8 oz	250 g	Leeks	
8 oz	250 g	Carrots	2. Sweat the vegetables in butter or olive oil in a stock pot.
4 oz	125 g	Celery	
1/2	1/2	Garlic cloves	3. Add cold water and bring to a boil. Reduce the heat and simmer, uncovered, about 30 minutes.
8 oz	250 g	Mushrooms	
4 oz	125 g	Tomatoes	
3 pt	1.5 l	Water	4. Strain and cool.
1/4	1/4	Bay Leaf	
2	2	Peppercorns	
pinch	pinch	Thyme	
4	4	Parsley stems	

VARIATIONS

For a brown vegetable stock, sauté the onions until caramelized. Add the remaining vegetables and proceed as in the basic recipe.

Stock's flavoured with individual vegetables are made by the same procedure. Use a large quantity of the desired vegetable and omit the remaining vegetables in the basic recipe. Add fresh herbs and peppercorns as desired. In the case of mushroom stock and shallot stock, brown the vegetable well in butter or olive oil before adding the water.

FRESH EGG PASTA

Yield: 1 lb. 8 oz - 700 g.   Portions

US	METRIC	INGREDIENTS	PROCEDURE
1 lb.	450 g	Bread flour	1. Put the flour in a mound on a work surface. Make a well in the centre and add the eggs, oil and salt.
5	5	Eggs, lightly beaten	
1/2 oz	15 ml	Olive oil	2. Working from the centre outward, gradually mix the flour into the eggs to make a dough.
pinch	pinch	Salt	

3. When the dough is firm enough, begin kneading it, incorporating more of the flour. If the dough is still sticky when all of the flour has been incorporated, add more flour a little at a time. Knead well until the dough becomes elastic and fairly smooth.

4. Cover the dough and let it rest for at least 30 minutes.

5. Cut the dough into pieces about 6 to 8 oz each (175 to 250 g). Set the rollers of a pasta machine at the widest opening. Working with one piece of dough at a time, pass the dough through the machine. Fold the dough into thirds, then pass it through the rollers again without resetting the width. Continue rolling and folding, using the widest opening, until the dough is smooth. If the dough is sticky after rolling, dust it lightly with flour as needed. Repeat this procedure with the remaining pieces of dough.

6. Again working with one piece of dough at a time, decrease the width between the rollers by one notch and pass the dough through them again. Dust the dough with flour as necessary to keep it from sticking. Repeat the rolling procedure, decreasing the width by one notch each time, until the dough is as thin as desired.

VARIATIONS

Chanterelle Fettuccini—For each pound [450g] of flour, use 5 eggs and 1 to 1 1/2 oz [30 to 45 g] of dried chanterelle, ground into a fine powder. If the dough is too dry, add an additional egg yolk or two or a little beaten egg.

Herb Pasta—Arrange whole herb leaves, such as flat-leafed parsley, chervil, or tarragon, at intervals on a sheet of rolled-out pasta. Top with another sheet and press down firmly. Pass the double sheet again through the rollers.

HERB OIL

US	METRIC	INGREDIENTS	PROCEDURE
		Fresh Herbs, as needed Olive oil	1. Drop the fresh herbs into boiling water. Blanch for 10 seconds. Drain and refresh under cold water. Drain again and pat the herbs dry with towels.
			2. Put the herbs in a blender and add a small amount of olive oil. Blend to make a paste.
			3. Remove the paste from the blender and measure its volume. Put in a jar and add four times its volume of olive oil. Shake well and let stand.
			4. After 30 minutes, put the jar in the refrigerator.
			5. The next day, filter the oil through a paper coffee filter.

VARIATIONS

Dill, Arugula, Basil, Tarragon, Chervil, Cilantro.

SOY MILK & BLACK WALNUT BISQUE WITH ROASTED BROCOVERDE

Yield: 4 Portions

US	METRIC	INGREDIENTS	PROCEDURE
			Mise en Place:
2 oz	60 g	Onions	1. Chop the onions.
2 oz	60 g	Butter	2. Toast the walnuts in a hot oven for a few
1 oz	30 g	Flour	minutes. Cool and grind them.

US	METRIC	INGREDIENTS	
1 pt 12 oz	9 dl	Vegetable stock	
6 oz	200 g	Black Walnuts	
1-2 oz	30-60 g	Roasted Walnuts for Garnish	
6 oz	2 dl	Soy Milk	
6 oz	2 dl	Heavy cream	
		Salt	
		White Pepper	

Cooking

1. Cook the onions slowly in the butter or olive oil without letting it brown.
2. Add the flour to make a roux. Cook the roux but keep it white.
3. Whip in the stock. Bring to a boil. Add the ground walnuts and simmer 20 minutes.
4. Strain the soup through cheesecloth. Squeeze the solids in the cheesecloth to extract all liquid.
5. Reheat the soup. Heat the soy milk and cream and add them to the soup. Season.

VARIATIONS

Other nuts, such as hazelnuts, pecans or English walnuts, can be substituted for the Black walnuts.

ROASTED BROCOVERDE

US	METRIC	INGREDIENTS	PROCEDURE
1 small	1 small	Brocoverde Olive oil Season to taste	1. Leave the brocoverde in a whole piece. 2. Coat the brocoverde with olive oil to help prevent sticking and reduce drying. Baste several times during cooking if required. 3. Roast in 350°F or 175°C oven till done.

Plating Procedure

Pour the bisque into broad soup serving dish, garnish with pieces of roasted florets of brocoverde, sprinkle with roasted walnuts and chopped fresh chives. *Optionally*, make a brocoverde or cauliflower timbale [see recipe pg. 39] and unmold in the centre of the plate, and finish presentation as above.

ROASTED SUMMER SQUASH SOUP WITH SPAETZLE & HERB BUTTER
Yield: 4 Portions

US	METRIC	INGREDIENTS	PROCEDURE
4 oz	125 g	Onions	**Mise en Place:**
1/2 oz	15 g	Butter	1. Chop the onions. 2. Cut summer squash in half and place on a greased tray and roast in oven at 350°F or 177°C till done. 3. Slice the bread and fry the slices in butter until golden brown on both sides.

US	METRIC	INGREDIENTS	
2 oz	6 cl	White wine	**Cooking/Finishing:**
1 1/2 pt	75 cl	Vegetable stock	1. Cook the onion slowly in the butter without browning
10 oz	300 g	Summer squash meat	2. Add the wine and vegetable stock. Bring to a boil.
			3. Add the browned croutons. Simmer until the vegetables are tender. Then add the roasted summer squash.
			4. Purée the soup.
2 oz	30 g	French Bread	5. Heat the cream and add it to the soup.
1 oz	60 g	Butter	6. At service time, garnish each portion with hot spaetzle and cold herb butter pieces.
2-4 oz	6-12 cl	Heavy cream	
Garnish:	*Spaetzle*	*Herb Butter*	

SPAETZLE

US	METRIC	INGREDIENTS	PROCEDURE
2	2	Eggs	1. Beat the eggs in a bowl and add the milk or water, salt, nutmeg and pepper.
1/2 cup	125ml	Milk or water	2. Add the flour and beat until smooth. You should have a thick batter. If it is too thin, beat in a little more flour.
1/3 tsp.	1.5ml	Salt	3. Let the batter stand 1 hour before cooking to relax the gluten.
pinch	pinch	Nutmeg	4. Set a colander [or spaetzle machine, if available] over a large pot of boiling, salted water. The colander should be high enough so that the steam doesn't cook the batter in the colander.
pinch	pinch	White pepper	5. Place the batter in the colander and force it through the holes with a spoon.
5 oz.	150g	Flour [or more]	6. After the spaetzles float to the top of the water, let them simmer a minute or two and remove them with a skimmer. Cool quickly in cold water, and drain well.
			7. Cover and refrigerate until service.
			8. Sauté portions to order in butter until hot. Serve immediately.

HERB BUTTER

US	METRIC	INGREDIENTS	PROCEDURE
		Fresh Herbs, to taste	1. Soften the butter by working it in a mixer or food processor.
4 oz	125g	Butter	2. Blend in the flavouring ingredients.
			3. Roll the butter into a cylinder about 1 inch [2.5 cm] thick in a sheet of parchment, wax paper or plastic film. Chill until firm. Slice off portions and cut into cubes to drop on top of the soup.

Plating Procedure

Pour soup into broad serving dish, arrange pieces of spaetzle over it and dot with cold herb butter.

Optionally, make a squash timbale [see recipe pg. 39] and unmold in the centre of the plate, and finish presentation as above.

VEGETABLE RAVIOLI IN GINGER BROTH AND CURRY OIL

Yield: 4 Portions

US	METRIC	INGREDIENTS	PROCEDURE
6 oz	175 g	Chinese cabbage	1. Prepare the vegetables: Shred the cabbage. Cut the scallions into thin slices. Cut the mushrooms into julienne. Trim the snow peas and cut diagonally into julienne.
3	3	Scallions	
2 oz	60 g	Shiitake mushroom caps	
2 oz	60 g	Snow Peas	
1 oz	30 g	Vegetable Oil	2. Heat the oil in a sauté pan over moderate heat. Add the vegetables and ginger. Sauté until the vegetables are wilted.
1/4 tsp.	1 g	Grated fresh ginger	
2 tsp.	10 ml	Sherry (optional)	
1 tsp.	5 ml	Vegetarian type oyster sauce	3. Add the sherry and the oyster sauce. Continue to cook until the vegetables are tender and there is no liquid in the pan.
1/2 tsp.	3 ml	Sesame oil	
1 tbsp.	3 g	Cilantro, chopped	
		Salt	4. Remove from the heat and cool. Add the sesame oil and the cilantro. Season with salt.
8 oz.	250 g	Fresh Herb Pasta dough in thin sheets [**Basic Recipes**— Fresh Egg Pasta— Variations Herb Pasta]. Water or egg wash, as needed	5. Lay out half the pasta sheets on the worktable. Place mounds of the vegetable mixture about 3 to 4 inches (8 to 10 cm) apart on the pasta, using about 1/2 oz (15 g) for each mound.
			6. Brush the exposed pasta with water or egg wash. Top with the remaining

sheets of pasta. Press the two layers of pasta together to seal them, at the same time pressing around the vegetable mounds to eliminate air bubbles. Cut into round or square ravioli.

7. In a saucepan, simmer the stock with the ginger slices until reduced by half. Strain and season with salt

US	METRIC	INGREDIENTS	PROCEDURE
10 oz	3 dl	Vegetable Stock	**Finishing:**
6-8	6-8	Fresh ginger slices	1. Drop the ravioli into boiling salted water. Reduce the heat and simmer about 3 minutes, until the pasta is cooked.
		Salt	
		Cilantro and curry oil for garnish	2. Remove the ravioli with a skimmer and drain well.

CURRY OIL

US	METRIC	INGREDIENTS	PROCEDURE
3 tbsp.	20 g	Curry powder	1. Mix enough water into the curry powder to make a paste.
1 tbsp.	15 ml	Water [approximately]	2. Transfer the mixture to a jar and add the oil. Shake well.
1 pt	5 dl	Flavourless oil	3. Let stand at room temperature for 1 day. Shake several time.
			4. When the oil has taken on enough flavour, filter through a paper coffee filter. Store the oil in the refrigerator.

Plating Procedure
Arrange the ravioli in broad soup plates and pour the ginger-flavoured stock over them. Garnish with a few leaves of cilantro and drizzle with some curry oil.

CORN & LEEK PANCAKES WITH A GREEN LENTILS SALSA & PEAR JUICE REDUCTION

Yield: 4 Portions

US	METRIC	INGREDIENTS	PROCEDURE
4 oz	125 g	Leeks, white part only	1. Cut the leeks in half lengthwise and wash well. Slice crosswise into very fine slices.
4 oz	125 g	Frozen corn kernel, thawed & chopped	2. Sweat the leeks in the butter until the leeks are tender add the corn and cook

1 oz	30 g	Butter	until all moisture has evaporated.
1	1	Egg	3. Cool completely.
		Salt	4. Beat the egg in a bowl.
3 1/2 oz.	100 g	Flour	5. Sift the flour. Beat the flour, egg, and
2/3 cup	160 ml	Milk	milk together to make a thin batter. Stir in the leek & corn mixture.

Cooking:

1. Heat a nonstick pan over moderately high heat. Spoon 1 tbsp. (15 ml) of leek & corn batter on the pan to make a small pancake. Cook until set and lightly browned on the bottom. Turn over and cook a few seconds on the other side.
2. Repeat with the remaining batter.

GREEN LENTIL SALSA

US	METRIC	INGREDIENTS	PROCEDURE
4 oz	125 g	Green (Le Puy) Vegetable stock (as needed)	1. Soak the lentils in cold water for several hours or overnight. Drain & rinse.
1/2 oz	15 g	Butter or olive oil	2. Place the lentils in a pot with enough
1/2 oz	15 g	Shallot, chopped	stock to cover. Simmer just until tender
1 tsp.	3 g	Jalapeño, minced	but still whole. Do not cook until soft and
1 oz	30 g	Red bell pepper, small dice	broken up. Drain and spread out on a sheet pan to cool quickly.
1/2 oz.	15 g	Jicama or water chestnuts, small dice	3. Heat the butter or oil in a sauté pan. Add the shallot, jalapeño, and bell pepper.
		Salt	Sauté for 1 or 2 minutes, keeping the
		Pepper	vegetables somewhat crisp.
2 oz.	60 g	Fresh corn kernels	4. Add the jicama and corn. Cook another 1 or 2 minutes.
2 tbsp.	6 g	Cilantro, chopped	5. Add the lentils and heat through. Stir in
		Hot red pepper sauce	the cilantro.
			6. Season with a generous quantity of red pepper sauce (the dish should be spicy) and salt and pepper.

PEAR JUICE REDUCTION

US	METRIC	INGREDIENTS	PROCEDURE
1 pt	5 dl	Pear Juice	**Cooking:**
1 oz	30 g	Butter	1. Place the juice in a saucepan. Bring to a boil and reduce by half. Season to taste.
		Salt	2. Stir in the butter.

Plating Procedure

Layer alternatively pancake and salsa. Drizzle some salsa around the stack and coat with the pear juice reduction.

PAN FRIED POLENTA WITH GRILLED FIELD MUSHROOMS, PORT WINE REDUCTION

Yield: 4 Portions

US	METRIC	INGREDIENTS	PROCEDURE
20 oz	6 dl	Water	1. Measure the cornmeal, water and salt. The following quantities will produce the approximate yields indicated.
3/4 tsp.	4 g	Salt	2. Bring the water and salt to a boil in a heavy sauce pot.
4 oz	125 g	Polenta [Italian coarse-grained yellow cornmeal]	3. Slowly sprinkle the cornmeal into the boiling water, while stirring constantly. Take care to add the meal slowly enough so that lumps are avoided.
			4. Cook over low heat, stirring almost constantly, for about 15 to 20 minutes. Stirring not only helps the polenta cook evenly without lumping, but it also causes some starch to be released from the cornmeal into the water. This creates the proper texture.
			5. Polenta to be cooled and sliced should be slightly stiffer. When it is done, pour it out onto a lightly buttered sheet pan [or, if you want to avoid the butter, onto a sheet pan lined with plastic film]. With a spatula, spread it into an even layer of desired thickness. Cool. Cut into desired shapes. Grill or pan-fry.

SAUTÉED ZUCCHINI

US	METRIC	INGREDIENTS	PROCEDURE
8 oz	250 g	Zucchini Butter or Olive oil, as needed Salt & pepper, to taste	1. Cut zucchini into a fine julienne. 2. Quickly sauté the zucchini in a hot pan, season and serve at once.

GRILLED FIELD MUSHROOMS

US	METRIC	INGREDIENTS	PROCEDURE
8 oz	250 g	Portobello, Meadow or Prince mushrooms Sesame Oil, as needed	1. Brush sesame oil on both sides of the mushrooms, season with salt and pepper. 2. Grill mushrooms until tender. 3. Slice lengthwise.

PORT WINE REDUCTION

US	METRIC		INGREDIENTS	PROCEDURE
1 pt	1 strip	18 cl	Port wine	1. Combine the port, juice, and zest. Boil until well reduced and syrupy.
6 oz	1 1/2 pt	1 strip	Orange juice	2. Add the stock. Reduce by one-half.
		75 cl	Orange zest	3. Just before service, strain the sauce. Season to taste.
	5 dl		Vegetable stock	
			Salt	
			Pepper	

Plating Procedure
Mount sautéed zucchini in the centre of the plate, place a slice of polenta on top and arrange sliced mushrooms on the polenta. Drizzle the port wine reduction on the outer edge of the zucchini. *Optionally,* top potato ravioli with radish sprouts.

MUSHROOM FILLED POTATO RAVIOLI ON A BED OF MUSTACHE OF THE DRAGON

Yield: 4 Portions

US	METRIC	INGREDIENTS	PROCEDURE
1.5	1.5	Large russet [baking] Potato Vegetable Oil, as needed	1. Peel the potatoes. Using a mandolin or an electric slicer, cut lengthwise into paper-thin slices, as for making potato chips.
4.5 oz	135 g	Egg wash Mushroom Pasta Filling	2. Oil a baking sheet and arrange the larger potato slices on the sheet in a single layer.
			3. Bake at 400°F or 200°C until soft and still white, about 3 to 5 minutes. The object is to make them pliable enough to be folded without breaking. Remove from the oven and let cool, but do not let them dry out.
			4. Brush the potatoes with egg wash. Put 1 tsp. of filling in the centre of each slice and fold over to enclose the filling. Press down to seal the edges and to eliminate any air bubbles.
			5. Deep-fry at 350° to 375° F or 175° to 190°C until golden brown.

MUSHROOM FILLING

US	METRIC	INGREDIENTS	PROCEDURE
1/2 oz	15 g	Dried morels	Soak the mushrooms in hot water until soft. Drain and squeeze out excess liquid. Purée the mushrooms, gruyère cheese, and garlic in a food processor. Mix in the parmesan and parsley. Add enough heavy cream to make a smooth paste. Salt to taste. [*Note*: If a leaner filing is desired, use stock or mushroom-soaking liquid instead of heavy cream].
3 oz	90 g	Gruyère cheese	
1/4 tsp.	1 g	Crushed garlic	
1-2 oz	30-60 g	Parmesan Cheese	
1 tbsp.	3 g	Chopped parsley Heavy cream Salt	

WILTED MUSTACHE OF THE DRAGON

US	METRIC	INGREDIENTS	PROCEDURE
1 lb.	500 g	Pea shoots	1. In a frying pan add some oil when hot add in pea shoots and sauté till wilted.

SPICED CARROT JUICE

US	METRIC	INGREDIENTS	PROCEDURE
1/2 pt	2.5 dl	Carrot juice Salt	1. Place the juice in a saucepan. Season to taste. Bring to a boil
1 oz	30 g	Butter Garam masala	2. Stir in the butter and garam masala to taste and strain in cheese cloth.

Plating Procedure

Mount some wilted pea shoots in centre of the plate, top with ravioli and pour a pool of carrot juice around the pea shoots.

VEGETABLE TERRINE WITH SHIITAKE MUSHROOMS, TOMATO COULIS & DILL OIL

Yield: 4 Portions

US	METRIC	INGREDIENTS	PROCEDURE
1 lb.	450 g	Spinach	1. Have ready an appropriate mold. Use a 1 qt [1 *l*] triangular or horseshoe shape mold for the recipe. For ease of unmolding, line the molds with plastic film.
1/4 oz	7 g	Shallot, minced	
1/4 oz	7 g	Butter	
1 tsp.	4 g	Gelatin powder	
1 oz	30 ml	Vegetable stock Salt	2. Trim the stems of the spinach and wash it well in several changes of water. Cook in boiling salted water until done, about 2 minutes and drain. Rinse under cold water to cool, and drain. Squeeze dry.
2 oz	60 ml	Heavy Cream	

3. Chop the spinach into fine pieces by hand or in a food processor.

4. Sweat the shallots in butter until soft. Add the spinach and cook slowly until quite dry. Cool thoroughly but do not chill.

5. Soften the gelatin in the stock and then heat until it is dissolved. Cool and stir into the spinach. Season with salt.

6. Quickly whip the cream until it forms soft peaks. Immediately fold it into the spinach mixture. Pour it into the mold and smooth with a spatula. Chill until set.

5 oz	150 g	Cauliflower, trimmed	
2 oz	60 g	White turnips,pared	
1 tsp.	4 g	Gelatin powder	
1 oz	30 ml	Vegetable stock	
2 oz	60 ml	Heavy Cream	
7 oz	200 g	Carrots, trimed	
1 tsp.	4 g	Gelatin powder	
1 oz	30 ml	Vegetable Stock	
2 oz	60 ml	Heavy Cream	
		Salt	

7. Steam the cauliflower and the turnips until they are tender. Purée in a food processor. For the smoothest texture, force the purée through a sieve. Mix the two vegetables together. Heat slowly in a large sauté pan to dry out the purée slightly. Cool thoroughly but do not chill.

8. Repeat steps 5 and 6 to make the white mousse, pour it into the molds on top of the green mousse, and chill.

9. Trim, cook, and purée the carrots in the same way and dry the purée as above. Repeat steps 5 and 6 to make the orange mousse and add it to the terrine.

10. Unmold the terrines and slice to serve.

VARIATIONS

Other vegetable purées may be substituted for those in the basic recipe. For a low-fat version, omit the gelatin powder, stock and heavy cream. In place of the stock and cream use an equal quantity of strong aspic. Mix the aspic with the vegetable purée.

GRILLED SHIITAKE MUSHROOMS

US	METRIC	INGREDIENTS	PROCEDURE
8 oz	250 g	Large shiitake mushrooms Sesame oil, as needed	**Mise en Place:** 1. Brush sesame oil on both sides of the mushrooms, season with salt & pepper. 2. Grill mushrooms until tender 3. Cut into strips.

TOMATO COULIS

US	METRIC	INGREDIENTS	PROCEDURE
8 oz	250 g	Tomato, peeled, seeded and chopped Shallots, chopped fine	1. Combine the tomato, shallots, vinegar, in a blender and purée to a smooth consistency.
1 tsp.	3 g	Red wine	2. With the machine running, add the oil in a thin stream.
1/2 oz	15 ml	vinegar	
1	1	Egg yolks	3. If necessary, thin out the sauce with a little water or vinegar. Season with hot pepper, salt, pepper and extra vinegar if necessary.
8 oz	25 cl	Olive oil, or part olive oil and part salad oil Hot red pepper sauce or cayenne, to taste Salt Pepper	

DILL OIL

Refer to **Basic** recipes—Herb oil variation—Dill

Plating Procedure
Overlap two thin slices of the terrine in the centre of the dish, place the grilled shiitakes on one side of the terrine, pour the tomato coulis artistically around the terrine and shiitake, drizzle with dill oil.

ASPARAGUS RISOTTO WITH HAZELNUT OIL, RED WINE REDUCTION & ROASTED SHALLOTS

Yield: 4 Portions

US	METRIC	INGREDIENTS	PROCEDURE
			Mise en Place:
1/2 oz	15 g	Hazelnut oil	1. Heat the butter & oil in a large, straight
1/2 oz	15 ml	Oil	sided sauté pan. Add the onion & sauté
1/2 oz	15 g	Onion, chopped fine	until soft. Do not brown.
8 oz	225 g	Arborio rice	2. Add the rice and sauté until well coated with fat.
1 1/2 pt	7.5 dl	Vegetable stock, hot [approximate measure]	3. Using a 4 to 6 oz (1.5 to 2 dl) ladle, add one ladle of stock to the rice. Stir the rice over medium heat until the stock is absorbed and the rice is almost dry.
			4. Add another ladle of stock and repeat the procedure. Do not add more than one ladleful of stock at a time.
			5. Stop adding the stock when the rice is tender but still firm. It should be very moist and creamy, but not runny. The cooking should take about 30 minutes. The quantity of stock indicated is only approximate; you may need more or less. If much more is needed, water may be used for the additional quantity.
1/2 oz	15 g	Butter	6. Trim the bottoms of the asparagus spears
1 1/2 oz	45 g	Grated Parmesan Cheese	and peel the lower portion of the stems. Simmer until done. Cut into 1 inch [2.5 cm] lengths. Use the cooking water for
1 lb.	500 g	Asparagus	part of the stock. Chop the hazelnuts
1 1/2 oz	45 g	Hazelnuts	coarsely and toast them briefly in dry
		Salt	sauté pan.
			7. Remove from the heat and stir in the raw butter, cheese, asparagus and hazelnuts. Salt to taste. Serve at once.

RED WINE REDUCTION

US	METRIC	INGREDIENTS	PROCEDURE
1 pt 2 oz 1 1/2 pt 2-4 oz	5 dl 60 g 75 cl 60-125 g	Dry red wine Shallots, minced Vegetable Broth Butter (optional) Salt Pepper	1. Combine the wine and shallots and reduce au sec [until thick and syrupy]. 2. Add the stock. Reduce by one-third or desired consistency. 3. Strain the reduction. 4. Just before service, reheat the reduction and, if desired, monter au beurre. 5. Adjust the seasonings.

ROASTED SHALLOTS

US	METRIC	INGREDIENTS	PROCEDURE
12-20	12-20	Large shallots, as needed Oil Salt Pepper	1. Remove the outermost peel from the shallots but try to leave a little stem. Carefully cut off the root ends without cutting into the shallot. 2. Place the shallots on a sheet pan or other flat pan. Pour a little oil over them. Roll them around so that they are well coated with the oil. 3. Roast at 350°F or 175°C about 1 hour, until very soft.

Plating Procedure

Use a 3" circle to shape the risotto in centre of the plate, arrange asparagus on top of it and place the roasted shallots on the dish around risotto. Pour the reduction artistically around the risotto and dust with roasted nuts.

CHANTERELLE FETTUCCINI WITH A SMOKED TOMATO SAUCE & SWEET BASIL OIL

Yield: 4 Portions

US	METRIC	INGREDIENTS	PROCEDURE
12 oz	350 g	Chanterelle Fettuccine pasta [Basic Recipe—variation Chanterelle]	1. Drop the fettuccine into boiling salted water. As soon as the fettuccine is al dente [which should be about 1 minute after the water returns to a boil], drain it and refresh with cold water.

SMOKED TOMATO SAUCE

US	METRIC	INGREDIENTS	PROCEDURE
2 lb 8 oz	1250 g	Smoked tomatoes*	**Mise en Place:**
4 oz	125 g	Onion	1. Peel and seed the tomatoes. Chop coarsely. If using canned tomatoes, crush lightly and drain briefly in a sieve.
1 clove	1 clove	Garlic [optional]	2. Peel the onion. Cut into small dice.
1 oz	3 cl	Olive oil	3. Peel and mince the garlic.
		Salt	
		White Pepper	**Cooking:**
1/2 oz.	15 g	Butter [optional]	1. Heat the olive oil in a sauce pan over moderate heat. Add the onion and garlic. Cook slowly for 2 or 3 minutes, but do not let it brown.
		If not available use regular tomatoes.	2. Add the tomato. Simmer for about 15 minutes, until the tomato is soft and the juices are slightly reduced.
			3. Purée the mixture by forcing it through a sieve or food mill.
			4. If the sauce is too thin, return it to the saucepan and reduce it over moderate heat until it reaches the desired consistency.
			5. Season with salt and pepper
			6. Stir in the raw butter if desired.

ROASTED GARLIC

US	METRIC	INGREDIENTS	PROCEDURE
		Garlic heads as needed	1. Use whole heads of garlic. Do not separate or peel, but slice off the tops [stem ends] of the heads to expose the cloves.
		Oil	
		Water	2. Place cut side up on sheet pans, coat with oil and add about 1/2 inch [1 to 2 cm] of water to the pan.
		Salt	
		Pepper	3. Roast at 350°F or 175°C until soft.
			4. Blend into a smooth paste with some oil.

SWEET BASIL OIL

Refer to Basic recipes—Herb oil—variation Basil

Plating Presentation

Twist cooked fettuccini around a cook's fork into a haystack shape and place in centre of plate, pour tomato sauce around the fettuccini, spoon the roasted garlic purée and sweet basil oil on the tomato sauce. *Optionally*, add fresh sprigs of basil on top of fettuccini and / or sauce as well as strips of smoked tomatoes and pieces of black olives.

PORCINI BARLEY PILAF WITH CARROT CHIPS, PARMESAN LACE & HERB JUICE

Yield: 4 Portions

HERB JUICE

US	METRIC	INGREDIENTS	PROCEDURE
2 cups	50 cl	Mixed Herbs such as chives, basil, chervil, flat parsley...	1. Bring water to a boil.
			2. Blanch herbs for 1 minute maximum and quickly cool.
1/2 cup	125 ml	Water	3. Purée cooled poaching water and herbs in a blender. Season to taste.
		Salt	
		Pepper	4. Before service, heat the juice and monter au beurre.
2-3.5 oz	60-105 g	Butter	

PORCINI BARLEY PILAF

US	METRIC	INGREDIENTS	PROCEDURE
1/2 oz	15 g	Dried porcini mushrooms	**Mise en Place:** Soak the dried porcini in hot water until they are soft. Drain the mushrooms and squeeze them out, reserving all the soaking liquid. Strain or decant the liquid to remove any sand or grit. Chop the mushrooms.
2 oz	60 ml	Hot Water	
			Cooking:
1/2 oz	15 ml	Oil	1. Heat the oil in a heavy pot. Add the onion and celery. Sauté briefly.
2 oz	60 g	Onion, small dice	
2 oz	60 g	Celery, small dice	2. Add the barley and sauté briefly, as for making rice pilaf.
5 oz	150 g	Barley	
10 oz	3 dl	Vegetable Stock	3. Add the broth, and mushroom liquid. Bring to a boil. Stir in the chopped mushrooms. Add salt to taste.
		Salt	
			4. Cover tightly. Cook on top of the stove over low heat or in the oven at 325°F or 169°C, until the barley is tender and the liquid is absorbed, about 45 to 60 minutes.

CARROT CHIPS

US	METRIC	INGREDIENTS	PROCEDURE
1 medium	1 medium	Carrot Suggested amount only	Cut carrot into thin slices [lengthwise] and deep-fry until crisp. Cooking time is usually about 10 to 15 seconds.

PARMESAN LACE

US	METRIC	INGREDIENTS	PROCEDURE
		Parmesan Cheese	Shave lace from a parmesan block using a vegetable peeler or mandoline.

Plating Procedure

Mold barley pilaf into a 3" circle and place in the centre of the plate, arrange carrot chips and the parmesan lace on top, drizzle herb juice around the barley pilaf. *Optionally,* use porcini oil instead of hazelnut oil, arrange pieces of roasted porcini mushrooms around pilaf and drizzle with porcini oil on top of herb juice. Sprinkle with chopped fine herbs and cracked fresh pepper.

ROASTED RED PEPPERS ON A CELERY ROOT PURÉE WITH A CHAMPAGNE VINAIGRETTE

Yield: 4 Portions

US	METRIC	INGREDIENTS	PROCEDURE
1/2 lb.	250 g	Potatoes	**Cooking:**
1/2 lb.	250 g	Celery Root	1. Pare the potatoes and celery root. Boil or steam until tender.
2 oz	60 ml	Milk	
1 oz	30 g	Butter	2. Purée the potatoes and celery root with a food mill.
1 tsp.	1 g	Chives, chopped	
2 tsp.	2 g	Flat leaf Parsley, chopped	3. Heat together the milk and butter until the butter melts. Mix with the potatoes & celery root and add the chives & parsley.
1-4 oz	30-125 ml	Heavy cream Salt White Pepper	4. Add enough cream to bring the potatoes and celery root to the desired consistency. The purée should be soft and moist.
			5. Season to taste with salt & white pepper.

ROASTED RED PEPPERS

US	METRIC	INGREDIENTS	PROCEDURE
1 lb.	450 g	Red peppers	1. Wash the peppers. Leave them whole. 2. Char the peppers on a grill, over an open burner, or under a broiler. Continue until the skins are blackened al over but don't char them so much that the flesh is burned. 3. Wrap them in a plastic bag. This hold in steam, which helps to loosen the skins. Leave them in the bag for 15 minutes or longer. 4. Rub off the skins. Rinse briefly to remove all the blackened skin. 5. Cut the pepper in half lengthwise and remove the core, seeds and membranes. 6. Cut the peppers into strips.

CHAMPAGNE VINAIGRETTE

US	METRIC	INGREDIENTS	PROCEDURE
12	12	Pearl onion, roasted & chopped	1. Roast the pearl onion in the olive oil. 2. Combine the vinegar, champagne, salt and pepper. Stir to dissolve the salt. 3. Slowly add in the olive oil, then the chopped roasted pearl onions. 4. Taste for seasoning and adjust if necessary.
4 1/2 oz	15 cl	Olive oil	
Pinch	Pinch	Pepper	
1/2 tsp.	3 g	Salt	
3 tbsp.	50 ml	Dry Champagne	
1 tbsp.	15 ml	White vinegar	

Plating Procedure
Mold or shape the celery root purée into a 3″ circle or dome, top with the roasted peppers and spoon the champagne vinaigrette around the purée. Dust with coarsely chopped chervil.

FENNEL TIMBALE WITH CHRISTMAS, BUTTER & CRANBERRY BEANS & ROASTED TOMATOES

Yield: 4 Portions

US	METRIC	INGREDIENTS	PROCEDURE
14 oz	400 g	Seasoned Fennel vegetable purée	**Cooking:** 1. Mix the ingredients together.
2 oz	60 ml	Heavy cream	2. Butter the small timbale molds of 2 to 5 oz [60 to 150 ml] capacity.
3-4	3-4	Eggs, beaten	3. Transfer the timbale mixture to the molds. Do not fill them all the way to the rim because the mixture may expand somewhat as it cooks.
			4. Set the molds in a hot water bath and bake at 375°F or 190°C until set. This may take from 20 to 45 minutes, depending on the size of the molds, their spacing in the water bath, and other factors.
			5. When set, remove them from the oven. Let them stand 10 minutes to allow them to settle.
			6. The timbales can be kept warm for a short time in the water bath until service.

VARIATIONS

Other vegetable purées can be used for this recipe including cauliflower, broccoli, carrot, squash, red pepper, asparagus. For more stable but less delicate timbale, substitute béchamel sauce for all or part of the heavy cream.

CHRISTMAS, BUTTER & CRANBERRY BEANS

US	METRIC	INGREDIENTS	PROCEDURE
1/4 cup		Christmas beans	**Cooking Beans**
1/4 cup		Butter beans	1. Pick over to remove any foreign particles and rinse well.
1/4 cup		Cranberry beans	2. Soak overnight in three times their volume of water.
9 tbsp.		Mirepoix	3. Cook each of the beans separately. In each pot add 1 tbsp. oil and sauté 3 tbsp. of Mirepoix, add the beans and cover with water.
3 tbsp.		Oil	4. Simmer, covered, until tender. Do not boil, or the vegetables may toughen. Some beans require up to 3 hours of simmering.

FENNEL JUICE REDUCTION

US	METRIC	INGREDIENTS	PROCEDURE
1 pt	5 dl	Fennel juice	1. Place the fennel juice in a saucepan. Salt to taste. Bring to a boil and reduce to desired consistency.
		Salt	
2 oz	60 g	Butter	2. Stir in the butter.

ROASTED CHERRY TOMATOES

US	METRIC	INGREDIENTS	PROCEDURE
2 pt		Cherry tomatoes	1. Place the tomatoes on a sheet pan or other flat pan. Pour a little oil over them. Roll them around so that they are well coated with the oil.
		Oil	
		Salt	
		Pepper	2. Roast at 350°F or 175°C, until soft.

Plating Procedure

Unmold fennel timbale in centre of the plate, place the mixed beans and roasted tomatoes around timbale, spoon the fennel juice reduction on the beans. Dust with dill weed. *Optionally*, add some roasted mushrooms and decorate with fennel fronds.

Study Guide

Summary

What are some of the Vegetarian factors?

- People choose to become vegetarian because of ethical, religious, economical, environmental or health reasons.
- There are three types of vegetarians diets: Lacto-ovo, Pure or Vegan and Pesco - Semi or Partial, although the later is not a true vegetarian diet.
- A vegetarian diet provides many health benefits and may actually prevent or reduce the onset of certain diseases.
- Vegetarian food is often perceived to be boring, bland and lacking complexity and therefore is not as popular as it could be.
- Protein is the macro-nutrient that has a potential to be of concern for vegans.

Why is it important to identify vegetarian media?

- Vegetables, fruits, grains, herbs, spices and legumes provide a multitude of textures, flavours, colours, shapes including nutrients which are needed to create balanced vegetarian meals.
- Most chefs view vegetarian media only as a garnish or as a complement to animal protein, but not as the main menu component.
- A vegetarian chef palette is a helpful tool to identify and categorize media, their properties and the varieties or products available to create complex vegetarian meals.

What are the important factors that affect vegetarian menu composition?

- The chef must define what his/her customers needs are and create meals that reflect those concerns using approaches such as nutritional or health versus creative or gastronomic culinary values.
- Vegetarian media lack the flavour and mouthfeel of animal fat, but alternative cooking preparations can provide similar sensations.
- There are three guidelines to follow to create a nutritionally or gastromonically balanced vegetarian meal: varied preparation techniques, assorted textures, and interesting flavour combinations.

Terms for Review

Lacto-ovo
Pure Vegetarian or Vegan
Pesco and Semi or Partial
Protein
Essential Amino Acid
Protein Combining
Fat
Customers Needs
Vegetarian Chef Palette
Menu Creation and Preparation Techniques
Menu Theme
Menu Creation and Assorted Textures
Grading principles
Menu Creation and Flavour Combination

Self Assessment Questions

Selected Response Questions - True or False

1. People become vegetarian only because of health reasons.   T   F
2. A lacto-ovo vegetarian diet excludes the use of honey and gelatin.   T   F
3. There is no link between a nutrition and better health.   T   F
4. Amino acids make-up the long chain of protein.   T   F
5. A bowl of kidney bean chili with a bun provides a source of complete protein for vegans.   T   F

6. Vegetarian media are only used as garnishes.   T   F
7. One of the most important factor for a chef to meet is its customers needs.
                                 T   F
8. Each amino acid must be present in every meal.   T   F
9. A dish of steamed brown rice with boiled lima beans will provide gustatory, auditory and visual stimuli.   T   F
10 Flavour complexity is reached by juggling flavours that match or enhance one another.   T   F

Questions for Discussion

1. Name 3 attributes that vegetarian media provide.
2. Name 3 advantages of using a vegetarian chef palette.
3. What are the two approaches associated with the creation of a vegetarian meal.
4. Provide two examples of ingredients and cooking methods that provide similar flavour and mouthfeel as animal fat.
5. Give one meal example for each of the three guidelines used to create a nutritionally or gastronomically balanced vegetarian meal.
6. Create a 5 course gastronomic vegetarian menu and provide the rationale for your choice [answer each of the four steps proposed to compose a balanced vegetarian meal].

Resources & Directory

VEGETARIAN NUTRITION BOOKS

Dunne, L.J., 1990. *Nutrition Almanac—Third Edition.* McGraw-Hill Publishing Co.

Garrison, R.H., Somer, E. 1990. *The Nutrition Desk Reference.* New Canaan, Connecticut: Keath Publishing Inc.

Melina, V., Davis, B., Harrison, V. 1994. *Becoming Vegetarian.* Toronto: Macmillan Canada.

CONVENTIONAL VEGETABLE COOKERY BOOKS

Gisslen, W. 1992. *Advanced Professional Cooking.* New York: John Wiley & Sons, Inc.

Gisslen, W. 1999. *Professional Cooking, 4th Edition.* New York: John Wiley & Sons, Inc.

PLANT IDENTIFICATION BOOKS

The following is a good wild mushrooms identification book for beginners.

McKenny, M., Stuntz, D.E. 1987. *The New Savory Wild Mushroom.* Seattle: University of Washington Press.

SOURCE OF ORGANIC SUPPLIES

GrainWorks Inc., Box 30, Vulcan, Alberta. Canada T0L 2B0 Certified Organic supplier of many common as well as exotic grains, beans, rice & flours.

Canadian Organic Growers, PO Box 6408 Station J, Ottawa, Ontario K2A 3Y6 An organization that maintains a list of Canadian Certified Organic growers. Culinary—Baking Arts & Vegetarian Cuisine Educational Material & Services.

DC Duby Hospitality Services Inc., PO Box
63115—6020 Steveston Hwy., Richmond,
British Columbia, Canada V7E 2K0
Tel/Fax: 604-277-6102
E-mail: dcduby@helix.net
Web-site address:
www.lightspeed.bc.ca/dcduby/
Computer based learning material &
printed training modules, professional
development seminars, hospitality
educational and management training—
consulting services.